Praise for *Everybody Has a Book Inside of Them*

"Ann Marie Sabath's book inspired me to transform myself from someone who has always dreamed of writing a book 'someday' to actively engaging in the process of unleashing the book inside of me. A truly thrilling journey!"

—Laura Davis

"Anyone with a story to tell will benefit from *Everybody Has a Book Inside of Them.* And that's just about any of us. Ann Marie provides answers to questions for both the novice wordsmith to the accomplished novelist-to-be. Her experience as a successful writer is invaluable in helping others understand the true 'ins and outs' of the writing world."

—Jordan Rich, cofounder, Chart Productions,
host of *On Mic with JR* podcast,
WBZ Boston Radio personality

"When you read *Everybody Has a Book Inside of Them,* you will feel like you are attending a writers' conference for budding authors. I was so motivated by the sage advice that I actually began writing my book!"

—Elaine Chambers

"*Everybody Has A Book Inside of Them* encourages readers to stop hiding behind their own story. It shines light on the writing process and how others have done it which proves that you can do it, too."

—Michaela Lehner,
creator of Dare To Be You Summit

"I was so inspired by Ann Marie's new book *Everybody Has a Book Inside of Them* that I started making my own list of questions and introspection to help me get organized and to start thinking about what I know best and what I am most passionate about . . . and I realized, wow, I can be an author!"

—Tara Low, founder/Editor-in-Chief
Guitar Girl magazine

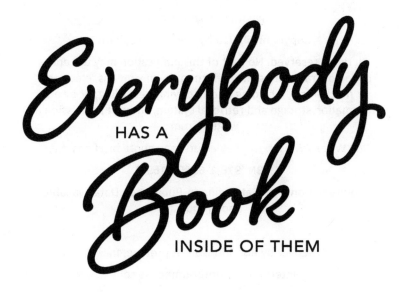

Everybody
HAS A
Book
INSIDE OF THEM

How to Bring It Out

Ann Marie Sabath

Author of *What Self-Made Millionaires Do That Most People Don't*

CAREER PRESS

This edition first published in 2019 by Career Press, an imprint of

Red Wheel/Weiser, LLC

With offices at:

65 Parker Street, Suite 7

Newburyport, MA 01950

www.redwheelweiser.com

www.careerpress.com

ISBN: 978-1-63265-169-3

Library of Congress Cataloging-in-Publication Data available
upon request.

Cover by Rob Johnson, Toprotype, Inc.

Interior by Scriptoriumbooks.com

Printed in the United States of America

_____

10 9 8 7 6 5 4 3 2 1

*Start telling the stories that only you can tell,
because there'll always be better writers than you
and there'll always be smarter writers than you.
There will always be people who are much better at
doing this or doing that—but you are the only you.*

—Neil Gaiman

Dedication

*To my parents, Mary and Camille Sabath, who took
their unwritten books with them.
To my children, Scott and Amber, who are living the
stories they have yet to tell.
To my granddaughters, Sonya and Catalina, who I
hope will someday put their thoughts on paper to share
with future generations.*

Acknowledgements

To Michael Pye, my associate publisher, who believed in this book enough to make it a Career Press title.

To Laurie Kelly, the director of sales for Career Press who reminds me that bottom-line book selling is the name of the game.

To Michael Conlon, the production manager who continues to score home runs when it comes to meeting book printing demands.

To Lisa Barretta, Susan A. Berger, Jan Cullinane, Allana Da Graca, Cornelia Gamlem, Marie D. Jones, Maryann Karinch, Lydia Lambert, Gail Z. Martin, Barbara Mitchell, Ken Murray, Erica Orloff, John Pierce, Herb Reisenfeld, and Kris Spisak, who shared their expertise for budding readers in this book.

To Allan Schiller, my personal mensch and *Ahuvi*, who has been both a wonderful cheerleader and sounding board advisor throughout this project.

To Laura Schiller, my substantive editor and sounding board advisor who guided me from the inception of this book idea to its finished product.

To Elaine Stone, my developmental editor and sounding board advisor who sensitized me to the wants and needs of budding authors.

To Rob Johnson, my newly adopted bro and president of Toprotype, who designed the book cover and was a true pleasure to work with.

To Suzy, my business partner, who has stuck with me through thick and thin, and helped me to turn in this book manuscript early!

And of course, to Mozart, my Maltese, who warmed the hearts of many and became the catalyst for writing this book.

Contents

Write!

Answers to Questions You May Not Have Thought to Ask!

In Retrospect . . .

Introduction: How This Book Came About

To produce a mighty book, you must
choose a mighty theme.

—Herman Melville

The act of us meeting through this book is magical. While I did not realize it at the time, a series of events led me to write *Everybody Has a Book Inside of Them*. Below is the sequence of events that inspired it.

On January 1, 2018, I turned in the manuscript for my ninth book, *What Self-Made Millionaires Do That Most People Don't*. On May 21, the book was released in bookstores and on Amazon, and on June 1, Mozart, my six-month-old Maltese and I started on a seven-month book tour journey.

Mozart and I traveled around the country meeting bookstore employees whom I consider to be "the aunts and uncles" of my books. We did forty-five signings in bookstores as far west as Seattle, Washington, and as far east as Framingham, Massachusetts. We visited an additional twenty-five bookstores to meet more "relatives" and sign the inventory of my books in stock.

The ensuing conversations during those hundred hours formulated the catalyst for this book. Here is how it happened.

Bookstore customers flocked to the signing table—though it wasn't to see me; it was to meet Mozart. After three signings, the picture became clear: I wrote the book and Mozart was the one selling it!

Who would have thought? I had a new book marketing teammate and didn't even realize it!

More often than not, the dog-loving customers would ask to pet Mozart. They would ask to hold Mozart. The same people would even ask if they could take a selfie with the fluffy ball of fur. Note: My condition for these requested photo ops was that they would post the pic of "the dog that sells books" on their social media sites, as I would on mine.

When they handed Mozart back to me, they would ask in an almost obligatory manner, what prompted me to write *What Self-Made Millionaires Do That Most People Don't.* I would tell them and then in the next breath say, "Everybody has a book inside of them. What is yours?"

Several would blurt out the book topic they wanted to write. Their subjects ranged from memoirs, historical fiction, romance, and fantasy novels to self-help books. When I asked what was keeping them from writing it, many said they wouldn't even know where to start.

Other customers would respond, "I have to give that some thought." My ready response to them was, "It's not the answer; it's the question. Everybody has a book inside of them."

Regardless of their responses, these bookstore customers often were curious about the process of writing a book, which generated even more inquiries about my experience. Their questions included:

- How long did it take to you to write this book?
- Did you ever have writer's block?
- How did you name your book?
- Was your book ghostwritten?
- How did you discover your writing voice?

✕ Did you use a pen name?

✕ Were you trained as a writer?

After hearing these same questions repeatedly from individuals whom I began to label as budding authors, I realized that there was a need for this book. I also recognized that my answers to those questions would provide you, the reader, with only one perspective. For that reason, I reached out to fifteen authors who generously agreed to have their writing journeys included in this book.

You will learn what inspired these individuals to write their first books, how they found their writing voices, and what keeps them motivated to write. You will also read where and for how many hours per day or per week they write. In addition, they share with you their secrets for how they eliminate those dirty writing doubts from their minds, and what advice they would have wanted to be told as their younger writing selves.

As of this printing, these fifteen individuals and I have collectively written 193 books. Our books represent forty-three genres ranging from arts and photography; biographies and memoirs; business and money; computers and technology; engineering and transportation; fairy tales; folk tales and myths; lesbian, gay, bisexual, and transgender; literature and fiction; medical; mystery; thriller and suspense; parenting and relationships; political and social sciences; reference; religion and spirituality; romance; science fiction and fantasy; self-help; and travel.

Although our subject matter and writing styles vary, we share two common threads: our passion for writing and the once-upon-a-time dream to write a book. In each case, our dreams became reality.

Yours will too, when you bring that book out in you!

Get Ready!

Are You Ever Too Young or Too Old to Write A Book?

If you're a singer, you lose your voice. A baseball player loses his arm. A writer gets more knowledge, and if he's good, the older he gets, the better he writes.

—Mickey Spillane

How would you answer that question? My response is: Are you kidding? Of course you can write, no matter what your chronological age is. Writing is a timeless and ageless experience. You can and should begin to write that book inside of you the moment your urge for writing strikes.

According to Data USA (the most comprehensive and visualization engine of public US government data), the average age of writers and authors is 42.6 years. Based on this government data, the average age of male writers and authors is 44, and the average age of female writers and authors is 41.7.[1]

Who wants to be average, however? Set statistics aside and start writing when your moment of inspiration emerges. Herb Reisenfeld, one of my fifteen author colleagues in this book, did exactly that. He began writing his first book, *Checking Inn: The Adventures of a Tour Director* at seventy-five years of age. Two years later, it was published.

The following examples are two role models who set their ages aside. Instead, they listened to their inner voices regarding when it was time to bring out the book in them. In fact, both of them defied the age odds by being the youngest and the oldest individuals to author a book.

Take Anaya Lee Willabus, native of Brooklyn, New York, who launched her writing career in May 2015 when she was eight years old. By publishing *The Day Mohan Found His Confidence,* Anaya became the youngest person in the United States to publish a chapter book.[2]

Then there is Bertha Wood, who began writing her first book, *Fresh Air and Fun: The Story of a Blackpool Holiday Camp*, at the ripe age of ninety. She published this book based on her memoirs at one hundred and has been recognized by the Guinness Book of World Records as the oldest author to have first published a book.[3]

Reflection: How old are you going to be when you take the writing plunge?

Why Write a Book in the First Place?

Writing is like sex. First you do it for love, then you do it for your friends, and then you do it for money.

—Virginia Wolf

I doubt that you need to be convinced to write a book, otherwise you would not be reading this book in the first place. The more important question is: What will it take for you to make writing a book a priority in your life?

Putting your thoughts on a computer screen or paper is a terrific way to enhance both your personal and professional success. Below are the nine top reasons why people write a book. Which one(s) do you relate to?

1. You want to share your expertise with the masses.

You can work twenty-four-seven, yet only reach a limited number of people. Rather than hoarding what has taken you years to learn, writing a book allows you to share your knowledge with others all over the world.

2. A book acts as your legacy.

Five generations from now, most of us may not be known by even blood relatives. By writing your memoir or documenting what you know about your parents and grandparents in the form of a book, you will be leaving a paper trail about yourself for future generations. Second to leaving a large inheritance, a book describing your family roots will be seen as a treasure.

3. A book will help you to brand yourself.

Besides acting like a big business card, writing a book can help you to create your brand. Whether it is a service or product you represent, a book makes a great public relations tool.

4. A book can generate additional income.

Whether you are an introvert and simply want to stay in your writing zone or choose to get involved with a speakers' circuit, a book can and will generate income. And I can tell you firsthand, no matter how large or small the royalty check you receive, it makes great passive income.

5. You will form new relationships.

Writing a book can become more than a revenue opportunity. If you are an extrovert like me (I admit to being type A squared), you will have reasons to form relationships with other writers. Socialization is key to living a healthy life. And meeting like-minded people is definitely intellectually and emotionally stimulating.

6. You will put your writing skills to good use.

I bet you already spend a large percentage of each day writing email messages, texts, and maybe even a few hand-written notes now and then. Why not minimize that type of communication and put your writing skills into practice in another way? You guessed it! By bringing out the book inside of you.

7. Writing a book can act as a health tool.

Many authors use writing as a form of therapy. How smart is that? They divulge what they have experienced in life, how they managed the situation, and share the happily-ever-after results in book form. Talk about turning a negative into a positive!

8. You will fire up your neurons.

Writing is a terrific way to keep your brain in shape. You are forced to think about what you want to write and then put your thoughts into words. Before long, you may have enough pages for a book.

Note: The new minimum length for ebooks on Amazon is 2,500 words. As a point of reference, the word count for this book is 34,772 words—so keep writing.

9. You will meet your new best friend.

Yes, you really will—your writing voice. It has been waiting for you to invite it into your life. And if you play your writing cards right, it will become your lifelong partner.

If none of these nine reasons speak to you, I have one more: Why not write a book just for the fun of it? No editing, no marketing, nada! Just for pure enjoyment.

Reflection: Give thought to which reason(s) you will choose to write a book.

Do Your Market Research

Research is formalized curiosity, it is
poking and prying with a purpose.

—Zola Neale

People are my business. When I was doing market research for this book, I chose the people closest to me: my family.

I started the loosey-goosey, nonscientific research by sharing with each of my ten family members on a one-to-one basis that I was writing *Everybody Has a Book Inside of Them*. The only reason I was sharing this news with them was to hear their answer to the question, "So, what is the book inside of you?"

Three of them said, "Gosh, I never thought about it. Let me give that some thought." Four of the ten defensively proclaimed, "What are you talking about? I don't have a book inside of me! Quit trying to impose your love of writing on us!"

I had gotten exactly what I wanted: their reactions! Although they may not have realized it, my antagonistic self loved their responses, to which I calmly said, "It's not the answer; it's the question. Everybody has a book inside of them. *Think about it.*"

If you have ever met me, then you know that I cannot—as they say—*let a sleeping dog lie.* During separate follow-up one-on-one conversations with four of them, I asked, "So have you given thought to the book inside of you?" Here were their responses:

"Actually, I started writing a book a year ago. Would you like to see my draft?"

"I did think about it and have realized that my book has not yet surfaced."

"I never thought about writing a book until you asked. Mine would be an analysis of how five violinists interpret the same composition based on their own musical style."

"You have hounded so much to write a book that you brought one out in me. It is: 'Why I Don't Want to Write a Book!'"

This family member thought he was annoying me with his Seinfeld-like response, but it was brilliant! I egged him on, asking, "So what are you going to include in your 'Why I Don't Want To Write A Book!' book?"

His response proved that he *had* been giving thought to what might actually become a book by saying:

"I would divide the book into six sections:

What Prompted Me to Write This Book

Twenty Reasons Why You Should Not Write a Book

Three Benefits for Not Sharing Your Thoughts in Print

How to Shift Your Thought Gears If the Temptation to Write Strikes!

How to Ensure that Budding Authors Do Not Plagiarize Your Unwritten Thoughts

Why I Have Nothing Else to Say"

I told this writer-in-the-making family member why his book idea had the potential to be a best-seller. With eyebrows raised, he asked: "Seriously? Who would buy a book on why I don't want to write a book?"

My response: "For not wanting to write a book, you sure are interested!"

Whether the book inside of you is in the forefront of your mind, has not yet surfaced, or worse yet, has shown up and you are resistant to take that next step, you can be certain of one thing: *Everybody Has a Book Inside of Them* is for you!

Reflection: With whom will you share that you are writing a book?

How Long Does It Take to Write a Book?

I can write better than anybody who can write faster, and I can write faster than anybody who can write better.

—A. J. Liebling

When working with budding authors, this is the question that they ask during our first coaching session. I tell them that the question is as ambiguous as asking, "How long is it going to take me to travel from New York to Los Angeles?" when you have not decided on your mode of transportation. The answer will be different based on if you will be traveling by plane, train, bus, or camel.

My first eight books took me six months to write based on other family and work responsibilities. My ninth book, *What Self-Made Millionaires Do That Most People Don't*, took four months to write based on my publisher's deadline.

The book that you are reading now took me two months to write. I gave myself this self-imposed masochistic deadline and actually enjoyed writing it more than my first nine books. The pressure was on, and some of the best writing happens to me when I am on a short deadline. There's no time to put off for tomorrow what you *must* write today. Please keep that in mind for yourself.

Now, if you really want to do yourself in and write a book in under a month, pick up a copy of Ginie Sayles's book, *Writer's Block Is a Crock! Write a Book In 3 Weeks—Or Less!*

So back to giving you the answer about how long it takes to write a book. In order to give you the right answer, I need to ask you the following two questions:

1. When do you intend to begin writing your book?

Be sure to set aside the first thirty days to go into your incubation thinking period. See section "Your Thirty-Day Incubation Period: Preventing Writers' Block Before Beginning to Write."

2. How many pages do you envision your finished book to be?

The last person with whom I spoke answered, "I intend to have my 180-page, single-spaced book finished by December 30." The date of that coaching conversation was on January 9.

Here is the formula I gave him for making his manuscript a reality by October:

If his 180-page, single-spaced book has approximately 250 words on a single-spaced page, his book would contain approximately 45,000 words.

A new author typically writes between 200 and 400 words an hour. Let's give this budding author some slack and say he is going to write only 200 words an hour. So, if you are like him, you will be scheduling seven one-hour writing appointments with yourself and dedicating seven hours a week to write. And if your goal is to have a 45,000-word manuscript composed of 180 single-spaced pages, it will take you about thirty-two to thirty-three weeks to write your book.

Let's say, however, that you commit to writing 400 words an hour rather than 200 words an hour for seven hours a week. You do the multiplication: That means you will be writing 2,800 words every seven days. In that case, it will take you approximately sixteen weeks to finish your 45,000-word manuscript. That means you will have accomplished your book-writing goal in four months!

By achieving your deadline early, you will have underpromised and overdelivered on bringing that book out in you! Now if that is not exciting, tell me what is!

Reflection: What is your beginning date for bringing out the book inside of you? It does not matter whether it is this year or five years from now.

You Never Know What the Catalyst Will Be for Motivating You to Write Your First Book

Everybody walks past a thousand story ideas every day. The good writers are the ones who see five or six of them. Most people don't see any.

—Orson Scott Card

Believe it or not, my love for writing began the day my parents took me to Dr. Sweeney's office to have the wart on my left foot removed. I was nine years old and scared to death of doctors due to the horrific experience I had three months prior when I had my first decayed tooth filled.

The merciless dentist filled my tooth without using an anesthetic. Between the shrill sound of the drilling and the terrible nerve pain, I was so scared that I poked a hole (a nice-sized one, I might add) into the dental chair in order to keep from screaming.

Consequently, my parents had to pay for my tooth being filled *and* a new chair for the dentist. I would have personally fired him if he had asked us not to return.

So, when my parents made me go to another doctor, a podiatrist, I immediately assumed that I was not going to like him. My first visit, however, started out on the right foot. Even as a child, I sensed that Dr. Sweeney had a wonderful chair-side manner. Since he did not hurt me, we got along great. I spared his leather chair (and my parents' wallets) by not poking a hole in it. Instead, I sat calmly as he examined the wart on my left foot.

I actually looked forward to each appointment with Dr. Sweeney. After the fifth visit, I was so enthralled with him that I went home and wrote a poem, which my mom mailed to Dr. Sweeney the next day.

During my follow-up visit to his office, I noticed a newly framed piece on the wall of Dr. Sweeney's waiting room. It was the poem I had written him in cursive and was prominently displayed for all of his patients to see. It went like this:

I had a foot doctor,
His name was Dr. Sweeney.
The first time I went to him,
I thought he was a meanie.
The second visit there,
He was very nice.
I thought he was made,
Of sugar and spice.
The third visit there,
He made me wait a while.
I really did not mind,
When he greeted me with a smile.
The fourth visit there,
Was as nice as before.
This time he greeted me,
As I walked in the door.
I was happy Dr. Sweeney,
Made my wart disappear,
Now I understand,
Why he is seen as such a dear.

So, there you go. Corny or not, keep an open mind and realize that your writing career can surface anytime, anywhere, and at any age.

Reflection: When did your love for writing begin? Think back to a very happy or sad experience. Relive it by writing about it.

From Writer to Author: The Steps for Getting There

The art of writing is the art of applying the seat of your pants to the seat of your chair.

—Mary Heaton Vorse

Rome was not built in a day. Neither will your book. You may have much of your book written and don't even realize it. For instance, if you have written a poem or a blog or have kept a journal, there's a better chance than not that you have poured out your heart on a topic that is important to you.

Here are three author scenarios in which this very thing happened:

Allana Da Graca began writing in 1999 as a student journalist with the UMass *Daily Collegian*. In 2006, she published her first booklet, *Temple: Self Discovery Through Truth.* She knew that she had "author" as her middle name, which gave her the impetus for writing her first book, *Tomorrow Can't Wait: An Inspirational Book Offering Persistence for a Lifetime* in 2014.

She continued to put her writing to good use and wrote volumes one and two of her Women Build Confidence coaching series. Allana shared that the inspiration for both the confidence-building series and *Chronicles of a Poet* came from the *Green Book*.[1]

As the author of *Kissing Frogs* puts it, "Journals are a wealth of book material." This writer put her more than twenty-five years of journaling to good use. In fact, she poured out her heart journaling as she tried to decipher how her Barbie and Ken marriage could dissolve. Years later, the savvy person behind the pseudonym of Lydia Lambert decided to make lemonade out of lemons by repackaging, expanding, and reexamining her dating experiences into *Kissing Frogs: The Path to a Prince.*

Finally, if you are a blogger, then you will identify with this author. Kris Spisak started blogging weekly in 2012. Her followers loved her posts on the art of communication so much that they encouraged her to write a book and include her most well-received blogs.

In 2015, Kris did exactly that, self-publishing an ebook. Shortly after this project began to find success, she gained both a literary agent and a traditional publishing deal. Her first traditionally published book, *Get A Grip on Your Grammar: 250 Writing and Editing Reminders for the Curious or Confused,* was published in 2017, and it includes much of that first indie published project that came from her blog.

Just as the title of Karen Carpenter's song goes, "You've Only Just Begun," so has this author. Kris Spisak has multiple books forthcoming, including an examination of the language of food called *Not to Mince Your Words* and her first novel.

So now that you have heard a few of the steps that took these individuals from writer to author, dig out those articles that you have written, journals you have kept, and blogs you have posted. Evaluate the hot spot, the common thread about which you have written.

Do you remember the poem you wrote about the girl on your school bus when you were in the first grade, the love letter to the boy who was your first crush, or the "My

Mother, My Hero" report you wrote as a high school English assignment? It just may be the topic for that book inside of you!

Reflection: Give thought to what you have written over the years, which may just become the catalyst for your book.

What Prompted Other Authors to Write Their First Books

You can't wait for inspiration. You have to go after it with a club.

—Jack London

Is it the first story written and stapled together in elementary school? Is it the first time they finish a full manuscript, even if the manuscript ends up being nothing more than a learning exercise? Or is their first book the first professionally edited and published work that has their name on the cover?

—KRIS SPISAK, AUTHOR, *GET A GRIP ON YOUR GRAMMAR*

When you read the above quote, did it make you question whether you already have written your first book yet did not label it as such? As you have heard me say throughout this book, it is not the answer; it is the question. You may want to schedule time to give thought to your answer.

Meanwhile, read on to learn the catalysts that brought out the books in ten other fellow authors. I am confident that their sage advice will take you a few steps closer to doing the same.

As Gypsy Rose Lee would say, let me introduce you to Lisa Barretta:

> Writing a book was never on my bucket list for things to accomplish. Ha! I guess you can say that inspiration is birthed from frustration. I had been working as an astrologer and intuitive tarot counselor for years, and I realized that a lot of people have no idea how to really get a good intuitive consultation. Additionally, conversations with my peers turned into "psychic shoptalk" that further inspired me to write a book about psychic readings from the perspective of the psychic. Some of the situations people get involved in are absolutely wild. My first book, *The Street Smart Psychic's Guide to Getting a Good Reading,* is more or less a very tongue-in-cheek look at the psychic profession as told from the other side of the tarot cards. Writing this book was actually very cathartic for me.
> —LISA BARRETTA, AUTHOR,
> *CONSCIOUS INK: THE HIDDEN MEANING OF TATTOOS*

> I was anticipating my fiftieth birthday and have always been mindful that both my father and mother died before their fiftieth birthdays. I never expected to live that long myself. It made me want to explore the significance of my perception of life span, as well as the sadness I always carried with me due to their early deaths.
> —DR. SUSAN A. BERGER, AUTHOR,
> *THE FIVE WAYS WE GRIEVE*

> My goal was to write an all-inclusive, holistic guide about retirement that would help the almost eighty million Boomers through this transition. There were retirement books that addressed the financial aspects; books that dealt with relocation, staying

healthy, and working after a primary career; with life transitions such as divorce and death and aging and caregiving; but there wasn't a book that had all this information in one nice package. As a Boomer, and as a spouse who had moved several times because of corporate transfers, I also knew I would personally benefit from my own research. I asked a friend, Cathy Fitzgerald, if she wanted to accompany me on this journey. She did, and is the coauthor of my first book, *The New Retirement: The Ultimate Guide to the Rest of Your Life*.

—JAN CULLINANE, COAUTHOR,
THE SINGLE WOMAN'S GUIDE TO RETIREMENT

A colleague and I wanted to write a guide for our clients, and the idea for a book emerged. We turned out something useful, but it never took off beyond our client base. We didn't know how to market it; this was before social media. Eight years later, another colleague had her book proposal accepted and invited me to coauthor it with her. I've been writing ever since.

—CORNELIA GAMLEM, AUTHOR,
THE CONFLICT RESOLUTION HANDBOOK

I have been writing stories since early childhood. In my twenties, I began writing screenplays too, but I still hadn't finished a novel. In my thirties, I got the bug to write a nonfiction book, a short and fun bit of spiritual commentary called *Looking for God In All the Wrong Places,* which led to my current status of having over sixteen nonfiction books in print. But my real love remained novels. Finally, about ten years ago, I sat down and wrote two novels in a row by participating in NaNoWriMo—National Novel Writing Month. I ended up with two lousy first drafts, but both are now edited; one is self-published, and the other will be traditionally published in 2020. It's a long and winding road for some of us, but as long as we get there. . . .

—MARIE D. JONES, AUTHOR,

THE DISASTER SURVIVAL GUIDE: HOW TO PREPARE FOR AND SURVIVE FLOODS, FIRES, EARTHQUAKES, AND MORE

While with Apple, as PR manager of their Federal Systems Group, I had great success promoting the use of Apple portable technologies in medical environments. A telemedicine team from Walter Reed Army Medical Center took a PowerBook, satellite communications unit, and digital camera— all separate items back in 1993—to Somalia during Operation Restore Hope, and I got lots of print and TV coverage. These docs saved huge amounts of taxpayer money on medical evacuations because they could do remote consults with specialists back at WRAMC. For example, a soldier with a rash near his eyes was diagnosed by the field doc as having lupus and was about to be evacuated to Landstuhl, Germany, to the army hospital there. By viewing images transmitted from Somalia, a dermatologist at WRAMC concluded it was much more likely to be contact dermatitis from the goggles the soldier was wearing to block the sand from his eyes. He was able to return to duty promptly. My understanding is that one incident alone saved the United States of America about $80,000. *I was obsessed with how important these developments in remote consults were for the future of health care.* (I bolded this sentence because it's the short answer to the question.) When Apple had massive layoffs in the Federal Group— almost everyone was let go—I was out of a job and decided to write a book about telemedicine. It was

published in 1994, and since then, I've had thirty books commercially published by houses of all sizes.
—MARYANN KARINCH, AUTHOR,
TELEMEDICINE: WHAT THE FUTURE HOLDS WHEN YOU'RE ILL

I wrote my first book at eight. It was about a pig with a curly tail, and I illustrated it myself! That was when I fell in love with writing. Publishing a book was always high on my bucket list, so when a colleague asked me to coauthor a book in 2008, I said yes and haven't looked back.
—BARBARA MITCHELL, AUTHOR, *THE BIG BOOK OF HR*

My external executive coach told me that after more than twenty years in financial services, it was time to give back.
—JOHN PIERCE, AUTHOR,
SELL MORE AND SLEEP AT NIGHT: RELATIONSHIPS WITH EMOTIONAL INTELLIGENCE TO INCREASE SALES

I had many adventures while being a tour director for over forty-five years in the travel business. Some were with famous personalities and many were very funny.
—HERB REISENFELD, AUTHOR, *CHECKING INN*

My first traditionally published book, *Get a Grip on Your Grammar: 250 Writing and Editing Reminders for the Curious or Confused,* all began from a blog I had started for some writing friends and editing clients. My goal was to break down grammar rules, communication strategies, and techniques for powerful storytelling into bite-sized, playful snippets, but I didn't originally have any big plans for the project. My big plans had always been for my fiction. But when my blog statistics showed spikes up to 15,000 users in a single day, I realized I might have something worth pursuing. After my readers convinced me to independently publish a collection of my top posts, it became the publishing story I didn't even dare to dream about. One success led to another, and I signed with my literary agent and was offered a traditional publishing deal shortly thereafter. *Get a Grip on Your Grammar* was the book I wasn't initially trying to write, but my passion for my subject matter found its way to a publishing deal. Passion can lead to great things, sometimes whether we intend it to or not.

—KRIS SPISAK, AUTHOR, *GET A GRIP ON YOUR GRAMMAR*

Now that you have read the myriad of reasons that the ten authors were driven to write their first books, I hope that you will take a deep look within yourself to see what the catalyst will be for bringing out the book in *you*. And don't wait too long. The story of how Ken Murray lost his father before he could share his story should remind you that if you have a story to tell, you should not wait. Time is not always on our side.

On a lighter note, before you read the next section, I have a favor to ask of you: Please put on your future "to-do list" that you will pay it forward. By that I mean after you write your first book, you will be as generous with your time as these authors have been by sharing their first book inspirational stories with you.

Reflection: What is going to prompt you to write your first book?

What Is Your Excuse?

A writer can write anywhere.
—Jerry B. Hawkins

Oftentimes, when traveling, I talk with strangers. Many of them are so interesting that I ask them why they have not yet written a book. Rather than me sharing the ninety-nine reasons that they have not written their book, let's focus on you. What is your excuse?

1. I have no idea where to start.

Come on, give yourself credit. You are reading this book, which means that you not only know where to start—you have already started! After all, the first step to doing what you don't know is to gather information and you are doing it. So, you can cross off that excuse.

2. I don't have the time to dedicate to writing a book.

If that is your excuse, then bringing out the book in you may not be a priority—for now, at least. It is good, however, that you are reading this book so that you will know what to expect when writing yours becomes a priority.

Do yourself this favor: Beginning next Monday, track how you use your time for that week in one-hour increments. Then reassess what you can do more efficiently so you can block out that hour to write. Example: If you notice that you have gone to the grocery store three times during a seven-day period, reassess your shopping habits so that you only go once. I bet that will free up at least two extra hours. Hmmm. You may have more time than you think to dedicate to writing your book.

3. English was not my favorite subject.

So what? Many of us are much better at things than we were in high school. Did you know that Brian Tracy, author of over seventy books, failed English and did not even graduate from high school?[1] Give me another excuse.

4. I don't feel like I have an expansive enough vocabulary to write a book.

Unless you are planning to write a dictionary or thesaurus, simply write like you talk. Your readers will not be looking for fifty-cent words from you; they will simply be interested in what you have to share with them in an entertaining and informative way.

5. I would feel vulnerable writing a book.

If that is the case, think twice about your choice of topic. Rather than writing a memoir, consider a book on your area of expertise. One way to minimize feeling vulnerable is to hide behind a pen name. So now what is your excuse?

6. I do not have the discipline that it takes to write a book.

Did I hear your voice from afar saying that you don't have the discipline it takes to write a book? What do you have the discipline to do? Show up for work on time? Pay your bills on time? You indeed *do* have the discipline to do many things. So please give yourself credit. When it *is* your time to bring out that book inside of you, you will have the discipline it takes to write it.

If you have yet more excuses about why you have not yet brought out that book inside of you, do yourself a favor:

Invest in a copy of *No Excuses* by Brian Tracy. He will show you how to get off what he calls the "Someday Isle" and stop concocting reasons for what you think you cannot do—such as writing that book inside of you.

Reflection: What has been your excuse for not writing your book?

How to Identify the Book Inside of You

If there is a book you want to read, but it hasn't been written, then you must write it.

—Toni Morrison

In a May 26, 2011, article at *PublishingPerspectives.com,* guest contributor Justine Tal Goldberg quotes Joseph Epstein as saying that "81% of Americans feel that they have a book inside of them—and should write it. That's approximately 200 million people who aspire to authorship."[1]

My hunch is that the other 19 percent of Americans also have a book inside of them. The reason they have not yet found the book inside of them is that it has not yet surfaced. And the reason it has not yet surfaced is because they have not yet asked themselves, "What is the book inside of me?"

If you are part of the 19 percent and are curious about what the book is inside of you, here are a few ways to begin the process of pulling it out.

1. Ask yourself, "What is the book inside of me?"

Do *not* ask, "*Is there* a book inside of me?" Of course there is! Everybody has a book inside of them. My responsibility is to help you to bring it out.

Avoid fretting about the answer. It will come to you. Now let me ask you, "What is the question you are going to ask yourself?" You got it! It is: "What is the book inside of me?"

2. Write down the previous question and put it in your wallet, under your mattress, in your smartphone, and in your glove compartment.

The question "What is the book inside of me?" will remain in your subconscious.

Reflection: Listen to your inner voice. When the time is right, you will hear the answer to "What is the book inside of me?"

Pack Your Grab-and-Go Tote

Most of the basic material a writer works with is acquired before the age of fifteen.

—Willa Cather

Just as you pack your bag to go to work, to the gym, or on a trip, I encourage you to pack what I call "a writing bag." By having your tools prepacked, you can literally pick up your bag and go, rather than spend time to gather your wares prior to each writing appointment.

I can tell you firsthand that having your writing bag prepacked will act as a time efficiency tool even when you are traveling as short a distance as down the hall to your spare bedroom. Also, when you are on the go, keep your grab-and-go writing bag close. I can tell you firsthand that some of my best thoughts enter my mind when I am in an elevator, waiting for a flight, sitting in the waiting room at my dentist's office, and oftentimes, when in flight.

Here is what I carry in my writing bag:

1. Two iPads. While I key my book manuscript on my oldest iPad, I keep an extra one close at hand to do both research and as a back-up device.

2. Earbuds. Antisocial as I might look, this tool minimizes people striking up a conversation.

3. My iPhone. When I have twenty minutes or less available, I jot down thoughts for my book in the Notes app on my iPhone. Since it is connected to the iCloud, whatever I key into the Notes app in my iPhone is automatically synced between devices and is also available on my iPad.

4. Two power cords.

5. My Mophie with an extra power cord: the wireless charging base.

6. Two pens. I key with a pen in hand—holding it like the cigarette that I have never smoked.

7. A small notebook. Great for jotting down those aha! moments and thoughts in this book.

8. A few snacks. Almonds and dark chocolate squares—yum!

9. A bottle of water. Besides staying hydrated, drinking water helps me to think more clearly.

10. Business cards. Never leave home without them. When talking with someone for more than five minutes, I hand the person my business card. It contains my contact info on one side with the cover of my most recent book on the other side. This is good practice for what you will need to do after publishing your book and you begin marketing it. This "give your business card out" practice helped to sell more than 6,000 books within the first six months of the release of *What Self-Made Millionaires Do That Most People Don't.* If you do not have business cards, have them made now.

A Special Message for Writing Moms and Dads

Do not wait to bring out the book inside of you until one of the three tech tools shared by other family members is available for you. If you do, you may make it into the Guinness Book of World Records as the oldest person to write a book!

Instead, designate a laptop/iPad or whatever you use to be yours and yours alone for writing. Make certain that you make it clear that your tech tool is not to be shared with kids and their sticky fingers playing video games and watching YouTube.

Make your writing tool of choice something totally sacred for you that no one else is allowed to open and see what you're working on, or accidentally delete. It's happened before; please do not let this writing catastrophe happened to you.

Reflection: Designate a canvas or leather bag with handles as your grab-and-go writing bag. Jot down the writing wares that you will put in it.

The One-Minute Way to Identify Your Book Genre

Never write anything that does not give you great pleasure. Emotion is easily transferred from the writer to the reader.

—Joseph Joubert

While only you know that answer, I will help you discover it with the following question:

When you go into a bookstore or online to browse books, which is the section that you visit first? Is it the mystery, thriller, and suspense section; the one on biographies and memoirs; or the section on religion?

Better chance than not that the book inside of you is related to the book sections that you favor the most. If you enjoy visiting more than one section, you may be the author-in-the making who will write in more than one genre.

At least, that is how it works for me. Without realizing it, the ten books that I have written all fall into the categories of self-help, inspiration, and motivation. And since I was a teen, they have been my favorite book genres. To this day, my home library is filled with books on those topics.

Take a look at your home and ebook library. There's a good chance they will give you an idea about the book genre that is inside of you.

Also, make a list of the past twenty books you have read. As the saying goes, "like attracts like," and that includes the kind of books you read with the one(s) that may be inside of you waiting to come out.

Reflection: What are the book categories that are of most interest to you?

Your Thirty-Day Incubation Period: Preventing Writer's Block Before Beginning to Write

I always keep two books in my pocket.
One to read, one to write in.

—Robert Louis Stevenson

I am a firm believer in preventive medicine, and that includes not being exposed to writer's block. Believe me, this section alone will have been worth investing in a copy of the book!

First and foremost, recognize that writer's block is a mindset. Secondly, if you catch it, the best cure is to get over it—and fast!

I use reverse psychology by not allowing myself to begin to write when a new book idea is conceived. You read that right! When a new book idea is inside of me, ready to burst out, I actually tell myself that I am not allowed to begin writing it until a definitive date. Usually it is thirty days from the day the writing itch sets in.

I consider this my incubation phase. I forbid myself to let my fingers touch the keyboard, which actually stirs up that want-to-write urge. I *do* allow myself to jot down every thought that I intend to include in the book—and do they ever flow!

I keep notepads in my office, in the kitchen, on my nightstand, in my purse, and admittedly, even in the bathroom. Some of my best thoughts have even come to me in the shower. By having a notepad nearby (no, not *in* the shower), I can quickly jot them down while they are still in the forefront of my mind—even if I am dripping wet.

If you do not yet see the value of giving yourself a "not allowed to write time" before letting your fingers do the keying, try the following exercise.

Buy your absolute favorite nonperishable food—and keep it prominently displayed on your kitchen counter for one month. During those thirty days, no matter how tempted you are, do not allow yourself to eat even an itsy-bitsy teeny-weeny piece of it.

I assure you that you will begin to salivate each time you think about it or walk past that delectable food. Now are you starting to get the picture about how using reverse psychology will also work for getting yourself psyched to write? Before long, you will say, "Writer's block? What's that?"

Try it! You will you like it. I'm not talking about your favorite food. Rather, the way to psyche yourself for bringing out the book in you!

Reflection: Figure out the food that you are going to buy when your writing urge strikes!

The Value of a Sounding Board Advisory Group

All of us, at certain moments in our lives, need to take advice and to receive help from other people.

—Alexis Carrel

When writing my books, especially this one, I found it incredibly helpful to get feedback on my writing in progress. I accomplished this mission by sharing each manuscript section with three individuals (of different generations) whom I chose as my sounding board advisory group.

Two of the three individuals were selected based on their curiosity about the necessary steps from the time a book idea is conceived through how to manage your writing voice, or better said, what to do once your writing voice takes over. The third person was and still is my partner. Besides respecting his feedback, I wanted him to see what I was doing when I went into seclusion for several hours at a time.

As a budding author, I encourage you to select the sounding board advisors that work best for you. There is no right or wrong number. Once you begin writing, you may even find that you prefer utter secrecy until you are finished with your entire draft. If you choose to have sounding board advisors, make sure they are supportive.

The reason I choose three individuals of different generations was to get three completely different perspectives from three people who see, experience, and live their lives differently. By doing so, my hope was for this book to reach a variety of budding authors coming from different places than I had or would experience.

Once these three people agreed to be my sounding boards, I wrote each section as though I were explaining how to bring the books out in them.

When my three sounding board advisors received the first three sections, diplomacy (too much so for my liking) prevailed when they shared their critiques. Eventually, they became more candid with their feedback and even began editing my work. Once they realized how much I valued their suggestions, they were more open with their constructive feedback.

Getting three different perspectives was invaluable. Oftentimes, one of my three sounding board advisors would sensitize me regarding how what I had written could be more clearly stated, while another would share her perspective about why a paragraph was unnecessary. I remember when my third sounding board advisory member recommended a sentence structure that was more succinct.

When you get to the stage of selecting your sounding board advisors, do so with these three criteria in mind:

1. Choose three individuals who have a sincere interest in your book topic.

2. Ensure that their schedules allow them to provide feedback to you within seventy-two hours from the time they receive each section. This will allow you to do your second round of edits while those sections are still fresh in your mind.

3. Choose individuals whose perspectives will vary so that you get a wider range of opinions.

Here is what three of my author colleagues shared about who and why they chose their sounding board advisors:

I had a couple of "critical friends" who would listen to passages or read what I had written and **let me know if it made sense** and **how it made them feel and think**. Then I edited accordingly. We didn't always agree. And in the end, it was still my story.
—LYDIA LAMBERT, AUTHOR,
KISSING FROGS: THE PATH TO A PRINCE

I spoke with friends to run by ideas. With their encouragement, I developed confidence that I had something to say that was worthwhile and would help others.
—DR. SUSAN A. BERGER, AUTHOR,
THE FIVE WAYS WE GRIEVE

Ms. Margie Wetenkamp-Castle was a huge help with the project. She knew Ralph and is now the Wing Commander's executive assistant at Randolph AFB. As the book progressed, I would send her two or three chapters to get her thoughts, **ensuring it was readable**, and more importantly, **understandable from a non-Air Force or flier perspective**. A second editor was Lynn Gonzalez. You must have other sets of eyes look at your work as you, the author, can get bogged down and gloss over things.
—KEN MURRAY, AUTHOR, *ON PARR*

Reflection: Give thought to whom you will choose to be your sounding board advisors.

Get Set!

What Authors Wear When They Write

It's not the appearance that makes the man, it's the man that makes the appearance.

—Unknown

Although there is no prescribed attire for preparing to get in your zone, I do recommend that you put on clothes that make you feel comfortable as you prepare to write. I never consciously gave thought to what I was going to wear when writing my first nine books. However, looking back, I realize that I definitely had, and to this day wear, self-prescribed writing garb that I call my "Velveteen Rabbit clothes."

You know which ones I mean. They are the clothes that you put on within minutes of getting home from work when you expect to be alone for the rest of the day. They are the clothes that only your immediate family members see you wear. They are the nonrestrictive, comfy clothes that let your body breathe as you prepare to let your words flow. Yes, those are the clothes that I am wearing right now. I'm glad you cannot see me!

Finally, when asking my author friends to describe their writing clothes of choice, several freely admitted that their garb ranged from shorts and a t-shirt (no matter what the weather) to glamorous clothes to pajamas. One not-to-be-named author proclaimed that he enjoyed writing in his birthday suit. To each his own!

No matter what clothes you choose to wear, make sure they are comfortable. When your body is relaxed, your words will flow more freely.

Reflection: What do you consider to be your writing garb?

The Importance of Setting Your Writing Zone(s)

I have to get into a sort of zone. It has something to do with an inability to concentrate, which is the absolute bottom line of writing.

—Stephen Fry

Some authors have a designated spot where they write; usually, it is where their computer monitor and keyboard are stationed. Others use a laptop, which allows them to be more flexible about where they write.

My writing zone has always been everywhere and anywhere. I have written on planes, trains, and cruise ships. When I am home, I write in my office, the kitchen, the dining room, and oftentimes, in the attic.

Call me a writing nomad if you like. It works for me. In fact, my nomadic life has me writing the words you are reading at this very minute in a lounge chair by a pool. Aha! Thought that might help you to see the benefit of being adaptable with your writing zone locations.

Although there are no sacred places when it comes to *where* I write, I do have two writing zone constants:

1. The direction that I face. See "How to Identify the Direction of Your Writing Energy Flow."

2. The iPad that I use to write. You can bet your bottom dollar that I carry a back-up iPad with me.

Take a look at six of my author colleagues' writing zones:

It would be so romantic if I could tell you that I write my books while I was in a quiet bungalow by the beach. So far from the truth. I wrote my first book, *The Street Smart Psychic's Guide to Getting a Good Reading,* on an old desktop computer in my family room. I wrote my second book, *Transformation,* and my third book, *Conscious Ink: The Hidden Meaning of Tattoos,* on a laptop at my dining room table.
—LISA BARRETTA, AUTHOR,
CONSCIOUS INK: THE HIDDEN MEANING OF TATTOOS

I write in my library, at my desk, where I can look out the window.
—JAN CULLINANE, COAUTHOR,
THE SINGLE WOMAN'S GUIDE TO RETIREMENT

I spent a lot of time in Starbucks, my basement, and basically anywhere that offers inspiration as writing prompts to get me going.
DR. ALLANA DA GRACA, AUTHOR,
TOMORROW CAN'T WAIT: AN INSPIRATIONAL BOOK OFFERING PERSISTENCE FOR A LIFETIME

I write at my desk, watching horse racing (my second love) on breaks. I write notes and jot down ideas or edit my daily work sitting in the family room with my son, or in bed late at night.
—MARIE D. JONES, AUTHOR,
11:11 THE TIME PROMPT PHENOMENON: THE MEANING BEHIND MYSTERIOUS SIGNS, SEQUENCES, AND SYNCHRONICITIES

I wrote my first book flying on planes instead of watching movies or doing "work."
—JOHN PIERCE, AUTHOR,
SELL MORE AND SLEEP AT NIGHT: RELATIONSHIPS WITH EMOTIONAL INTELLIGENCE TO INCREASE SALES

I write where I can and whenever I can squeeze it in. If it means pulling out my laptop on a park bench in the ten minutes I have between engagements, that works too.
—KRIS SPISAK, AUTHOR, *GET A GRIP ON YOUR GRAMMAR*

So as you see, everywhere and anywhere is a perfect place to write. It's your choice. Find a place so that you have your zone established when your writing mood strikes!

Reflection: When your book is ready to burst out of you, where will your writing zone(s) be?

How to Identify the Direction of Your Writing Energy Flow

Where focus goes, energy flows.

—Tony Robbins

In which direction do you sit in order to best concentrate? Yes, I mean "sit." If you are not aware of the importance of positioning yourself, don't feel badly. I didn't either until 1994. That is when I subconsciously recognized that the direction I faced when sitting down to read, write, or concentrate on anything, for that matter, either helped my thoughts to flow or blocked them.

Here is how I discovered this positioning phenomenon: I had moved our five-year-old business into new office space consisting of 2,000 square feet. This space was divided into one 1,000-square-foot office and three other offices that were approximately 300 square feet.

As the business owner, I initially chose the largest office as my professional home. After a few weeks, however, I realized that I could not concentrate in that space for long periods of time.

In order to solve this lack of focus dilemma, I switched offices with two of my staff members. They were each very willing (who wouldn't have been) to give up their

300-square-foot offices in exchange for sharing the beautiful 1,000-square-foot, brightly lit office space.

In turn, my new business home became one of the 300-square-foot offices. The second adjoining office became our client conference room. Within the first week of relocating to my cubbyhole, I mean "intimate" office, I found myself concentrating for much longer periods of time, yet did not understand why. One of my team members made me aware that I was unknowingly following the principle of feng shui.

Although I was skeptical about her remarks, before long I realized that she was right. My concentration level continued to improve for longer periods of time. I attributed it to my desk being positioned to face south in the cozy office, which also allowed me to face the door when seated at my desk. I could have repositioned my desk to face south in the larger office space, but I would have been facing the wall with my back against the door.

That same year, I also discovered that when I was home and chose to do office work or pay bills at the kitchen table, I would migrate to the chair across from the spot where I sat during family meals. I soon realized that I had subconsciously selected that "work seat" because it also was facing south—the same direction that my desk faced in my cozy office where I could best concentrate.

As I sit at my dining room table keying the very section that you are reading now, I stopped to download the Compass app in order to see the direction that I am facing. Once again, without realizing it, I chose the chair that—you guessed it—is facing south!

Writing zones are different for each person. You may also find that the direction in which you are compelled to sit will shift based on *what* you are writing.

Here is one more perspective from one of my author colleagues:

I did the writing for all three of my books while I was facing west. It was an unconscious decision, but it was the direction that worked best for me. Now, interestingly enough, I remodeled my house and the energy inside totally shifted. I find that I now do all of my writing facing south. Facing west now makes me feel blocked. In ritual, the west direction supports our intuitive self. In hindsight, I can see how most of my writing while facing west most certainly was birthed from an inner knowing and into my higher self.

My writing while facing south seems to be more spontaneous. I write a lot of short articles. In ritual, south represents inspiration, passion, and change. It is a fire direction and is itself the direction of magic.

—LISA BARRETTA, AUTHOR,
CONSCIOUS INK: THE HIDDEN MEANING OF TATTOOS

Reflection: Whether or not you believe in energy flow, figure out the direction to sit that allows you to concentrate the best. It works!

Know Thy Reader

No one can write decently who is distrustful of the reader's intelligence or whose attitude is patronizing.

—E. B. White

Let me give you an essential tip for making your book a success: Know your reader. Just as you tailor your email and texts to the people reading your messages, your content should be written as though you have an emotional connection with the individuals who will be reading your book.

During each of the thirty-day mandatory incubation periods prior to writing each of my ten books, I figured out the kind of readers whom I wanted to attract. For example, before beginning *Everybody Has a Book Inside of Them: How to Bring It Out,* I identified two groups of readers:

1. Individuals who wanted to write a book yet did not know where to start.

2. Those who had not even entertained the idea that they had a story to tell.

The following points are six ways that I identified my readers before starting to write each book. Hopefully, one of them will create an aha! moment for you when you are ready to identify your readership.

When writing my first book, *Business Etiquette In Brief,* I wrote as though I were talking to the individuals in the business etiquette training sessions that I had presented during the first five years of growing At Ease Inc. Although I received rave reviews from program participants based on the content and engaging delivery style, I now realize that my writing style was the total opposite. It was pretty stiff!

Rather than engaging my readers throughout *Business Etiquette In Brief*, I wrote as though I were having a one-way conversation with them. The reason? I had not found my writing voice and was unknowingly scared to death of the writing process. In fact, I didn't even know that a writing voice existed.

I now realize that *if I had* written *Business Etiquette In Brief* as though I were addressing a group of program participants, my writing voice may have surfaced. And the six months of writing this book would have been more much more pleasant than the dreaded experience that I had each time I sat down to write.

Despite that, authoring this first book did three things for me:

1. It gave me the confidence that I could write a book.
2. It opened doors for many speaking engagements.
3. It generated twenty years of royalties with a traditional publisher.

When giving thought to my second book, *Business Etiquette: 101 Ways to Conduct Business With Charm and Savvy*, I felt more confident about writing it than I had with my first book. Since my program participants had grown to become individuals in the professional services industry (law firms, accounting firms, and investment companies), I took my readership bar to another level: individuals who were already sophisticated and wanted to confirm that they were doing business with finesse.

Although I had not yet found my writing voice, I was certain that what I would document in this book would have as much impact on individuals as what I incorporated into company training programs.

The readers for my third, fourth, and fifth books were easy ones to pinpoint as a result of my globe-trotting experience. They consisted of anyone who conducted business internationally and individuals who interacted with those people who had cultural nuances different than their own. Oh yes, the book series was *International Business Etiquette: Asia and the Pacific Rim; International Business Etiquette: Europe;* and *International Business Etiquette: Latin America.*

Although you may not be questioning how I identified my reader, I bet you are wondering who made me the expert on international courtesy. Good question! In addition to being exposed to cross-cultural experiences from the age of five, I had traveled the globe for both leisure and business for more than seventeen years.

The clincher for writing the International Etiquette book series was being sent around the world by American Express Bank to work with their private bankers. I had learned so much during my travels that I wanted to document my newfound knowledge in book form. My readers were identified in two groups:

1. Those who wanted to be proactive and learn how to appropriately greet, meet, converse, and dine with individuals of other cultures.

2. Individuals who had lost a piece of business because they assumed that potential clients of other cultures who spoke English as a second language also had a Western mindset. Wrong!

The readers I envisioned for my sixth book, *Beyond Business Casual: What to Wear to Work If You Want to Get Ahead* came about as business casual became the Friday attire in the mid-1990s. Even the most conservative companies had adopted what were called "dress down" days for employees. Many employees, however, misinterpreted this perk as wearing clothes that they would change into when they got home from work or to mow the lawn.

After conducting a study with human resource managers representing the top 100 Fortune 500 companies regarding businesses casual dress faux pas that they witnessed in their organizations, I began writing *Beyond Business Casual*. You can imagine that the readers I identified were twofold:

1. Human resource managers who wanted to drop the hint to their employees about the real definition of business casual.

2. Employees whose organizations did not have a documented business casual dress code in their policy manuals.

The readers for my seventh book, *Courting Business: 101 Ways for Accelerating Business Relationships*, were anyone and everyone who had selling as their middle name. Strangely enough, I did not have to figure out this audience. My banker—yes, my banker—identified my readers for me.

Dave called me one day and requested that I stop by the bank that week. Since curiosity killed the cat, I hightailed it to the bank later that day.

When Dave and I met, he asked me what I did to generate the deposits that we continually brought into his branch. I was totally befuddled by his question and responded with, "You know what our company does, Dave. We present business etiquette programs to individuals in the professional services industry." Dave's comment was, "Of course, I know that. What I want to know is *how* you get them to become your clients. In other words, what is your sales process?"

"What is my process?" I was stunned by his question and said, "I do what all salespeople do. I keep our firm's name in front of prospects and existing clients on a monthly basis. When meeting with them, I make a point of arriving early so that my prospects are never kept waiting. When promising them a proposal, I make a point of sending it to them early. Anytime my prospects or existing clients give me more than fifteen minutes of their time, I send them a follow-up note."

Dave's response was, "That is where you are wrong, Ann Marie. Most salespeople do not put the sweat equity into their game. I told our director of sales about the revenue you generate, and he wants you to address his team during an upcoming sales meeting."

One year after presenting ten courting business programs for this bank and their six affiliate banks, I started writing my book *Courting Business: 101 Ways for Accelerating Business Relationships*. Talk about an easy way to identify my readership! And an even better way to roll out another nationwide training program on this topic.

My eighth book, *One Minute Manners: Quick Solutions to the Most Awkward Situations You'll Ever Face at Work,* came about because I fell in love with the name. I envisioned my readers as the Millennial generation who wanted quick and crisp tips. So that is exactly how the book was written. It is composed of the 144 most awkward situations that anyone in business is likely to encounter with quick and easy one-minute solutions.

Finally, when giving thought to writing my ninth book, *What Self-Made Millionaires Do That Most People Don't,* I decided to tailor my writing voice to people who wanted to figure out how to create their own success. I intentionally incorporated that phrase in the book's subtitle. The reason: to draw individuals to the book who were interested in discovering what it takes to create their "it."

So, there you have it. I have given you the strategies for how readers were identified in each of my books. As you see, it is an essential factor to know before bringing out the book inside of you.

Reflection: To whom will you be writing when you begin writing your first book?

How to Name Your Book

Some authors choose their book titles before their books are written. Others wait until the manuscript is finished to name it.

For the past twenty-seven years, I have been compelled to name my nonfiction books *before* I begin to write them. I keep this naming process proprietary until it has been narrowed down to two titles. At that point, I reach out to my sounding board advisors (who have been sworn to secrecy) for help.

Whereas choosing some of my book titles took a while to figure out, other ones such as *Everybody Has a Book Inside of Them* was a no-brainer. This title was born in response to peoples' comments after learning that I had written ten books (a minuscule number compared to the seventy-six books that some of my author colleagues have written). My automatic response to "You have written ten books?" is "Everybody has a book inside them. What is the one inside of *you*?"

After saying what I considered to be my elevator script response at least 100 times and listening to the answers of these individuals, I knew that I had to write a book about how to write a book!

So, when *you* are compelled to write *your* book and are ready to name it (either before or after writing it) here are three KISS (Keep It Simple, Stupid) guidelines to consider:

1. Choose a catchy title. When it comes to a book, it *is* judged by its cover and a title that should be catchy. A perfect example of an attractive book title is *Make Your Bed* by William H. McRaven.

2. Create a subtitle that will motivate your potential readers to open your book. Analogy: A book title is like the steak with onions that you ordered (forgive me, vegetarians). The subtitle is the steak's aroma that makes you want to take that first bite. A subtitle is a terrific way to sell the sizzle of the book's content. It should tantalize readers to look inside the book. A great example is the subtitle for *Make Your Bed*. It is *Little Things That Can Change Your Life . . . and Maybe the World.*

3. Make sure that your book title is available. You, rather than your publisher, will own your book trademark and licensing rights to the title of your book. If you are under contract with a traditional publisher, the publishing company will most likely file the necessary paperwork to trademark your book. If you are self-publishing, contact the United States Patent and Trademark Office *(www.uspto.gov/).* Timing and close attention to detail are essential to this process.

In fact, if you are self-publishing, I highly recommend that you hire a trademark attorney. This individual will be well worth the investment and allow you to sleep at night. It also will ensure that a thorough trademark search has taken place before your federal trademark publication has been filed. Stay focused on what you do best: to bring out the book in you!

Your book's title may need to be cast in concrete if you are under contract with a publisher. The reason is, your book cover will be designed as you are writing your manu-script. It is really exciting!

Reflection: If you were to write your first book, what would you name it? Have a brainstorming meeting with yourself to create a list of potential titles. This way when you are ready to bring it out, you will have a running start!

Are You a Pantser or a Plotter?

Plot is the last resort of bad writers.

—Stephen King

Although you are the first person to know this—no kidding—I willingly admit that for the past twenty-seven years, I have felt very guilty about the way I structured, or shall I say, did not structure my first nine books. The reason: I *had* no structure, no outline, no diagram. Nor had I ever thought of using a book template, nor would I have even recognized one if it had flashed in front of me.

What I did know for certain before writing each book was:

✕ The title.

✕ The fifteen to twenty topics that would be included.

✕ My audience and how it would benefit them.

✕ How it would be different than other books written about the same topic.

A definitive outline would have made me feel boxed in rather than allowing my words to flow. I told myself that if I were writing a thriller or romance novel, creating structure would be a prerequisite. Was I ever wrong!

When doing research for this book, I read two articles about how Jane Graves, Stephen King, and Nora Roberts write. And then, I just so happened to listen to the

New Yorker Politics and More podcast on *WNCY.org* during which David Remnick interviewed Lee Child, the creator of Jack Reacher.

After discovering how these romance, mystery, and thriller novelists write, I realized that many authors, no matter what their genre, do not follow a book structure. In fact, some of them detest it.

I was relieved to learn that my lack of structure was actually the norm for a category of writers called *pantsers*. The term means that these bestselling authors whom you will read about in this section write by the seat of their pants—and laugh, if I might add, all the way to the bank.

That does not mean that they—or shall I now say *we*—are disorganized. Let's say instead that pantsers free-write. They, I mean we, follow our intuition about the book content as it is being written. If this becomes your writing choice, welcome to the Pantser Club.

If you are a *plotter,* your style is to map out your book content in outline form—but please do not look down on pantsers. It's simply how some people write, specifically, *kinesthetic* writers. You will learn more about us in the Fourteen Budding Author FAQs section about "The Psychology Behind the Writing Tools That Authors Use to Write."

Here are descriptions from bestselling authors who proudly categorize themselves as pantsers:

Jane Graves, author of twenty contemporary romance novels says, "I don't plan. I don't outline. I have hated out-lines since sixth grade geography and I can't do Roman numerals."[1]

Nora Roberts, one of the world's bestselling authors of more than 225 romance novels says that "she never knows where her story is going," that she "sits down at her computer to find out."[2]

Stephen King, in his seminal work *On Writing,* says the following about plotting: "Plot is, I think, the good writer's last resort, and the dullard's first choice."[3]

Lee Child, novelist and creator of Jack Reacher, shared that when he starts each book, he knows within the first seven words or the first paragraph if he is on track. He explained that he does not do research, has no charts on the wall, and has zero idea about what he is going to write.[4]

Now that I know there is actually a label for what I thought what was an unorthodox style of writing, I have officially dubbed myself a pantser. It is refreshing to finally be guilt-free about choosing *not* have structure when I begin writing my books.

If you are a pantser, I hope to have spared you years of expending the unnecessary energy that going with your writing flow is wrong. I did enough for both of us! If you are a plotter, keep creating those outlines. Whatever works is right!

Reflection: Are you a pantser or a plotter?

Outline, Anyone?

I always have a basic plot outline, but I like to leave some things to be decided while I write.

—J. K. Rowling

If you read "Are You a Pantser or a Plotter?," you know that writing this section is definitely going against my book-writing grain. After all, pantsers don't do outlines!

If you are a plotter, I owe it to you, however, to write this section. And pantser friends, before you skip over this topic, please read it. It is good to know how left-brained people operate. Even though you may not choose to do it, I want you to think of a book outline like a roadmap. It gives plotters the direction they need for staying on course.

Also, pantsers, an outline may not be your book development style, yet you may want to give thought to creating a flexible one. Besides helping you stay organized, it also will help you to prepare to play the outline formatting game if you intend to go the traditional publishing route. Acquisition editors will expect a book outline as part of your proposal.

If you are starting to get stressed, please stop. I will walk you through the entire process in my next book and even give you the proposals that I used for getting my ten books published.

Sorry to digress, plotters. Now, since you probably work best by following a book outline, here is what you will want to include:

- ✕ The title of your book
- ✕ What your book will be about
- ✕ How your books will be different than other books on the topic
- ✕ The introduction (what prompted you to write the book)
- ✕ Your credentials for authoring a book on your chosen topic
- ✕ Who your readers will be
- ✕ What readers will gain from your book's content
- ✕ Your target audience
- ✕ The name of your book sections
- ✕ The topics that you will address under each section
- ✕ What the book will do for readers
- ✕ If your genre is fiction, your plot, the characters, and their actions in your chapters

Reflection: If you are a plotter, create a detailed outline when you are ready to write your book. Pantsers—are you still there?

The Way to Let Your Inner Writing Voice Be Heard

To gain your own voice, you have to forget about having it heard.

—Allen Ginsberg

As you read in "Know Thy Reader," I struggled to write my first six books. The reason, I now suspect, was that I did not create the optimal conditions in which my inner voice could emerge.

Perhaps I could not hear it because I was so busy letting my *outer voice* do the talking that my *inner voice* could not get a word in edgewise. I'm a naturally talkative person, so it is sometimes a challenge for me to sit back and let my thoughts take shape. Or maybe it was because I was just not listening to the whisper of my *inner writing voice* because I was expecting to hear a holler instead.

While I may never know the answer, I encourage you to allow your inner writing voice to lead the way. You can do this by creating safe time and space for it to speak.

Here is how I now listen to my inner voice:

1. I create a totally quiet environment by tuning out noise pollution (people talking; music playing; Mozart, my spoiled Maltese, yapping, etc.). Often, earbuds or noise

cancellation machines help the cause. Paying a dog walker on occasion might help too!

2. I let my inner voice—my thoughts—know that I am ready to listen to it by scheduling this thinking time. Oftentimes, by creating this quiet environment, my inner writing voice speaks up. "What next," you ask? Easy! Simply put your fingers on the keyboard and your thoughts will turn into words on your screen.

Reflection: Which speaks louder: your inner voice or your outer voice? If it is your outer voice, make room for your inner voice to speak by taking time to think and letting it be heard.

The Importance of Beginning with the End in Mind

*The first sentence can't be written until
the final sentence is written.*

—Joyce Carol Oates

If you read my ninth book, *What Self-Made Millionaires Do That Most People Don't,* you may remember that one of the fifty-two secrets for creating your own success is to visualize what you want to manifest by beginning with the end in mind.

This same principle applies to what it will take for bringing out the book in you. In both cases, it begins with a mere thought.

When you are ready to write your book:

✖ Visualize what you want the end result to be.

✖ Visualize what you intend to write about.

✖ Visualize the name of your book.

✖ Visualize where you will write.

✖ Visualize what your writing schedule will be.

✖ Visualize the date that your manuscript will be finished.

✕ Visualize the sense of accomplishment you will experience.

✕ Visualize how your readers will benefit from your book.

✕ Visualize where it will be sold.

Have you gotten the picture? VISUALIZE!

If you have not yet integrated the *believing is seeing* practice into your life, this is a perfect time to start. I can tell you firsthand that you *will* manifest what you *visualize*. It is not a matter of if; it will happen. It is a matter of when.

If you have even one dirty doubt floating through your mind, read on. You will soon say, "I believe, I believe."

Before my first fiction novel, *The Summoner,* got published, I worried that might never happen. After all, that was the book I worked on for twenty years, from college into my forties, through marriage, children, moving, job changes. But my husband and my friends believed in me, and the book just wouldn't let me give up on it. I dispelled the doubts by keeping the end goal in mind.

Every time I went into a bookstore, I would find the shelf where the fantasy books were and where my last name would be alphabetically. I would push the other books to the side, and put my hand on the place where my book would be someday. For twenty years. And one day, I stretched out my hand, and touched the spine of my first novel. It was an awesome day!

—GAIL Z. MARTIN, AUTHOR,

THE ESSENTIAL SOCIAL MEDIA MARKETING HANDBOOK AND *30 DAYS TO SOCIAL MEDIA SUCCESS*

So, as you see, the act of visualizing is incredibly powerful. Gail Z. Martin can vouch for that. Since publishing her first book in 2007, Gail has authored seventy-six (you read it right, seventy-six) epic fantasy, urban fantasy, and steampunk novels. She also coauthored six fantasy books with her husband, Larry Martin. As though that weren't enough, this go-getter has also written four nonfiction books and coauthored a fifth one with Larry Martin. Better chance than not, Gail has only just begun!

Reflection: Begin visualizing so the book inside of you will become a reality.

Write!

When Your Writing Voice Starts Talking, Start Keying!

I write only because there is a voice within me that will not be still.

—Sylvia Plath

When I decided to write this book, something happened. After the thirty-day incubation period was up (see "Your Thirty-Day Incubation Period: Preventing Writer's Block Before Beginning to Write"), I started writing, and something amazing happened. I could not stop writing. I'm not kidding. The ideas flowed faster than I could key.

Two hours seemed like twenty minutes. There were many days when Allan would leave to play tennis and return home four hours later only to find me in the same place where I was when he left. Worse yet, I would still be in my pajamas with my hair plopped on top of my head and would be keying so fast that you would have thought my life depended on it.

If you think I looked glamorous, please don't ask Allan. He is too nice to say anything mean. I will tell you firsthand: *au contraire!* Truth be told, I didn't really care how I looked. My priority was to give my writing voice 100 percent of my attention.

When your writing voice starts talking, set everything else aside and go to your closest writing zone. Then document what your inner voice is saying before those magical thoughts are lost.

Reflection: Get ready to let your fingers do the keying when your inner writing voice speaks to you.

Write the Way You Live Your Life

It ain't whatcha write, it's the way atcha write it.

—Jack Kerouac

I have always thought that people who are good at managing their time also know how to manage their money. I never correlated people's writing styles, however, with the way they live their lives.

Let's go back to your school days. It is Friday, and your teacher knew how to ruin your weekend by telling you that the following Friday you would be tested on XYZ material. My question for you is: How did you prepare for the test? Did you say to yourself:

✗ Heck, the test is a week from now. I will study for it the night before the exam. I'm sure not going to ruin my weekend by studying for it.

✗ I will get started this weekend by scheduling an hour a day to prepare for it.

✗ I will look at my calendar so that I can build in study time for this test.

✗ I will use the spare time I have to review the material throughout the week.

Read on to see if you best relate to the style of the Master Crammer, the Take-Charge-of-Your-Time Person, the Map-It-Out Person, or the Go-With-the-Flow Being.

Let me give you descriptions of these four types of people to help you identify with your writing style.

The Master Crammer

Are you the type of person who waited until the night before a test to study? Although this may seem like a terrible way to retain information, a crammer operates well under pressure. In fact, a high school friend used to study for a test the night before and would ace it!

If you are a master procrastinator and put off what you do until the last minute, consider yourself the Master Crammer! This may also be your writing style. I hope you have low blood pressure . . .

The Take-Charge-of-Your-Time Person

Perhaps you thrive on keeping schedules, like my partner? He gets up at the same time each morning, eats the same thing for breakfast every day, exercises at the same time, and even goes to bed every night at the same hour. If you can relate to this description, like him, you are a Take-Charge-of-Your-Time Person. And writing your book will simply be one more thing that you will add to your established routine. You know the twenty-one-day drill: anything you do for three consecutive weeks becomes a habit.

The Map-It-Out Person

Take note of what you did during the past twenty-four hours. Do you live by a master calendar by designating specific time to certain tasks? If this describes you, you live your life proactively rather than in a reactive mode. When you begin writing your book, there's a good chance you also will set aside a specific time to write.

The Go-With-the-Flow Being

If you get psyched by reacting more than by acting (doing what is planned), you may thrive on living an impromptu life. For example, do you accept last-minute dinner invitations from friends? While some people may label you "impulsive," the term "spontaneous" may better describe you. Rather than trying to fit into someone else's mold about how you should live your life, be true to yourself. You may be the most creative of all types of writers.

So now that you have read each of my descriptions about how you live your life, let's figure out which one will also describe your writing style. If you said, "the Master Crammer," welcome to the ranks of people who put off until the last minute what others do today. If you see yourself as the Take-Charge-of-Your-Time Person, you are organized and map out your life. If the The Map-It-Out Person describes you, make room on your calendar to allot a specific time to write. Finally, if the "Go-With-the-Flow Being" description defines your style, you live your life with vim, vigor, and spontaneity.

Although the type of person you are does not matter, what does matter is for you to recognize that your writing style will most likely be the way you live your life.

Reflection: Which of the four writing styles define you?

Feed Your Inner Voice
with Writing Prompts

"Just living is not enough," said the butterfly, *"one must have sunshine, freedom and a little flower."*
—Hans Christian Andersen

Being a friend to someone is a two-way street, and that includes with your new best friend, your inner writing voice.

Before I ever heard of the term "writing prompt," I would rev up my creativity motor before each session with what I called "food for thought." If you have been to my home, you know that you will not be here for more than ten minutes without being offered food or beverage as a sign of hospitality. I extend the same welcome to my inner writing voice by offering it "food for thought." This sustenance is often a quote, a podcast, a blog, or a magazine article related to the topic that I have scheduled to write about that day.

Let me give you a few examples:

When writing my seventh book, *Courting Business: 101 Ways For Accelerating Business Relationships,* the writing prompts would consist of feedback from my past participant program evaluations on the same topic.

When writing the manuscript for *What Self-Made Millionaires Do That Most People Don't*, I often used *Entrepreneur* magazine articles as writing prompts. I choose this publication knowing that approximately 75 percent of self-made millionaires are entrepreneurs.

When preparing to write about staying psyched to write in this book, I went to *BrainyQuote.com* in search of a few motivational quotes. When the topic was "getting rid of those dirty writing doubts," I searched for a blog on the magic of believing.

So you see, the point to having a writing prompt is to inspire and prepare your inner writing voice for take-off.

Speaking of take-off, there is no better time than now to prepare you for a practice writing take-off. Here is a writing prompt assignment for you:

1. During the next twenty-four hours, schedule one hour to write.

2. Jot down the topic that you and your inner voice will discuss.

3. During your sixty-minute writing session, give your inner writing voice three writing prompts food for thought. You will be surprised where those prompts may lead you.

Are you wondering why I recommend three rather than one or two writing prompts? Just as many guests often refuse a beverage they are offered the first time out of politeness and sometimes the second time around, so may your inner writing voice. By the third time, both your guest *and* your writing voice are bound to accept your graciousness.

Your guest will enjoy what you have prepared as will your invisible friend—your inner writing voice. Before you know it, the food for thought you have offered will inspire your inner writing voice to create words that will flow from your fingers onto your computer screen or legal pad.

Reflection: What writing prompts do you foresee using when you begin to write your book?

Two Ways to Stay Motivated to Write

If my doctor told me I had only six minutes to live, I wouldn't brood. I'd type a little faster.

—Isaac Asimov

Like everyone else, budding and existing authors tend to stay motivated about getting their thoughts on the computer screen (or paper) in one of two ways: either through the *carrot effect*[1] or the *KITA effect*.[2]

Let me explain each of these motivation theories as it relates to bringing out the book inside of you.

The *carrot effect* means that you have a positive goal in mind. For example, the positive reinforcement for an author would be to see his or her book come to life in the form of a digital, paperback, and/or audio book. One other form of positive reinforcement is the advance check that is received after a book contract is signed and the royalty checks that will pour in after the book is published and you, the author, promote as though your life depends on it!

On the other side of the coin lies the KITA effect. Many writers—myself included—find this form of motivation extremely effective. The reason: *KITA* means a kick in the . . . pants (tactfully put).

When writing a book, the KITA effect will definitely have a major impact on you, especially when the scary word *DEADLINE* is in front of you! Your deadline date will and should remain in the forefront of your mind day and night.

I realize that we are not in therapy; however, I must confess that the KITA motivational force stays with me (please don't put the book down) until each manuscript has been edited and it has finally been sent to the person who is awaiting it, my senior editor. (Note: If you are self-publishing or writing a book before it has been accepted by a publisher, make sure that you have designated someone who will hold you accountable for your self-imposed deadline.)

Now that you have heard what will motivate you to write from me, here are six candid comments about what has kept my fellow authors motivated for staying on *their* writing course:

> Deadlines, deadlines, deadlines. When you're writing for a traditional publisher, you have a deadline incorporated into your contract so you have a legal obligation to meet. If you're not writing against a contractual deadline, having a self-imposed one is a good way to keep yourself on track and accountable.
> —CORNELIA GAMLEM, AUTHOR, *THE MANAGER'S ANSWER BOOK*

> I enjoyed the process, so I didn't have a motivation issue. I'm also lucky that I like deadlines, and a line from one of my graduate school professors rang very true for me: "Nothing concentrates the mind like a hanging."
> —JAN CULLINANE, COAUTHOR,
> *THE SINGLE WOMAN'S GUIDE TO RETIREMENT*

Honestly, I signed a contract to get the book done. On a lighter side, I also formed a relationship with my manuscript. I would think of it as a friend that I was talking to every day and kept the conversation going.

—Lisa Barretta, author,
Conscious Ink: The Hidden Meaning of Tattoos

Deadlines motivate me as does working with coauthors who are much more time driven than I am. I give them permission to keep me on task!

—Barbara Mitchell, coauthor, *The Big Book Of HR*

That's like asking how I stay motivated to take the next breath.

—Maryann Karinch, author,
Telemedicine: What the Future Holds When You're Ill

My motivation was knowing the impact that my book would have on the younger generation—and others who want to develop better business relationships to do well in life.

—John Pierce, author,
Sell More and Sleep at Night: Developing Relationships with Emotional Intelligence to Increase Sales

Reflection: What is the driving force that motivates you in your life? If may be the same thing that will also motivate you to write!

How to Keep Up Your Writing Stamina

To maintain success, stamina is more important than talent. You have to learn to be a marathon runner.

—Joan Rivers

I stay inspired by watching my manuscripts take on a life of their own. This manifestation usually happens within the first three weeks of writing my book.

Talking with people whom I envision as my readers also keeps me inspired. As you read in the introduction, when writing *What Self-Made Millionaires Do That Most People Don't,* I created every opportunity possible to ask individuals about the book inside of them. Oftentimes, they would tell me that they did not know where to start. In other instances, individuals explained that they had started writing a book, however, they needed guidance to make it a reality.

Let me tell you about a specific conversation with a budding author whose name is Rolando. As I was preparing to write the last 15,000 words of this manuscript, I went into seclusion for three days by checking into a hotel to have total quiet. When I checked into my room, I noticed that one of the lamps did not turn on. Within ten minutes, Rolando, the person in charge of room preventative maintenance knocked at my door with a light bulb in hand. After assessing the situation, he said that the lamp would need to be taken out of the wall and replaced. He asked when it would it would be convenient for me to have him do that.

Since the room had five other lights that worked, I told him not to bother. I explained that I was on a writing deadline. He asked what I was writing and I enthusiastically said, "My tenth book, *Everybody Has a Book Inside of Them: How to Bring It Out.*"

In the same breath, I asked this thirty-one year old, "What is the book inside of you?" To my surprise, he said, "I am writing a book to teach individuals how to take care of their own household tasks rather than paying to have them fixed. I know that I can write it; however, I have so many questions about the appropriate book length, how to rid myself of writing doubts, and the book-writing process itself."

We talked for a while, during which time I gave him the short-version answers to his questions.

Conversations like the one I had with Rolando keep up my writing stamina. And my first talk with him will not be the last.

Oh yes, did I tell you that I have committed to mentor this budding author? To think that it all started with a light bulb!

Reflection: Give thought to what you will do to keep your writing stamina high.

How Authors Dispel Those Dirty Writing Doubts from Their Minds

Learn to write. Never mind the damn statistics.
If you like statistics, become a CPA.

—Jim Murray

Although I have always been an extremely confident person, there are times when writing doubts creep into my life. Better chance than not, they will also visit you. As a matter of fact, those dirty writing doubts may even be what has kept you from writing the book inside of you!

Worry not, however; my seasoned author colleagues, first-time author colleagues, and I want you to know the following:

1. It is normal to have writing doubts.

2. How we dispel these evil thoughts from our minds.

Here is how four authors manage their moments, hours, and once in a while, even days of dirty doubts:

Do I suck? Can I write? Who the heck would want to read what I write? Am I good enough? I ask those questions every day, even now, after all the books I have published and all the readers I've found for them. It is natural and human to have doubts and feel like you aren't good enough or don't have anything important to say. The true test of a real writer is to develop a thick skin and a stubborn spirit, and make the decision to go for your writing dreams no matter what your inner critic says. I guarantee there is a deeper voice within you that is cheering you on, and that is your intuition, instinct, and authentic self. The ego is what trips us up by making us care too much about what others think, including our readers. If we write from that perspective, it is the kiss of creative death. Write because you can't imagine not writing. Tell the stories that you came here to tell. Do the best work and edit, edit, edit—and tell the inner and outer critics to go get a life of their own.

I dispel my writing doubts by sitting down and working every day. I write every day, even if just in my head. I read a lot. I talk a lot to other writers and belong to groups on social networking where I feel less alone and more supported. I have learned to ignore most of my doubts and criticisms that might stop me because I want this badly, and always have. Now, when the doubts arrive, I smack them down like a good game of "Whack-a-Mole."
—MARIE D. JONES, AUTHOR,
THE DISASTER SURVIVAL GUIDE: HOW TO PREPARE FOR AND SURVIVE FLOODS, FIRES, EARTHQUAKES, AND MORE

Writing authentically is exposure. I was afraid of what people would think because the person writing the book was not the person that most people know and see on a daily basis. So mainly, I was afraid of what people would think. Then, after I finished it, I was afraid I couldn't get it published.
—LYDIA LAMBERT, AUTHOR,
KISSING FROGS: THE PATH TO A PRINCE

I didn't want to come off as a joke by authoring a book as a nonwriter. I dispelled this dirty doubt by investing in an editor to professionalize my content without altering the heart of it.

—JOHN PIERCE, AUTHOR,
SELL MORE AND SLEEP AT NIGHT: RELATIONSHIPS WITH EMOTIONAL INTELLIGENCE TO INCREASE SALES

Moving from nonfiction business writing into creative nonfiction, which a colleague and I are doing, is like writing a book for the first time. You have to use different techniques, and you can't help but wonder, "What if nobody likes it?" or "What if it isn't good?" So, we started to study the craft of writing—reading periodicals about writing and attending conferences and lectures to understand more about storytelling. How to develop characters, story arcs, and tension in a story.

—CORNELIA GAMLEM, COAUTHOR, *THE BIG BOOK OF HR*

Now that you have learned how new and seasoned authors alike manage their writing vulnerabilities, let me give you two final tips that I employ to both minimize and manage those dirty writing doubts:

1. Surround yourself with people you want to be like.

As you prepare to bring out the book in you, be discriminating about what you read. Choose books written by authors whose writing styles you admire. The reason: In time, you will become the sum total of the four people with whom you spend the most time. And when those dirty doubts creep into your mind, remind yourself that doubt is a normal part of the writing process.

2. Live by this mantra: It is not the situation; it is how it is handled.

When your writing voice doubts itself, ask it to tell you *exactly what it is doubting.* Then write down the specific doubt and *shred those darn words into pieces.* If that dirty writing doubt still remains in your mind (and it probably will), write it down again and *shred it into pieces* again. Repeat this writing down and shredding process until that dirty writing doubt is totally dispelled from your mind! I can tell you firsthand that this process works.

You may need a ream of paper for writing down and then shredding those dirty doubts. However, I promise that eventually you *will* win out! Your confident writing voice will surface and *you* may even begin guiding budding authors about how to dispel their own writing doubts. After all, it *is* all about paying it forward!

Reflection: If you ever second-guess your writing ability, you now have solutions for taking control of it!

The Surefire Way to Rid Yourself of Your Writing Censor

Censorship is to art as lynching is to justice.
—Henry Louis Gates, Jr.

When was the last time you were talking to someone who interrupted you? I don't know about you, but when that happens to me, it breaks my train of thought.

When you get the urge to write, avoid allowing your inner censor to make you second-guess your word choices. If you succumb to it, your inner censor could easily derail your thoughts. Instead, just keep your treasure of thoughts flowing. Your will only know what is inside of you when you get it out, so just keep writing.

When my writing confidence needs a boost, I schedule an email meeting with one of more of my sounding board advisors. Their feedback provides an objective perspective about what I have written and my choice of words. I hope you will do the same.

When I am tired and my writing censor sneaks up on me, it often talks louder than my writing voice. When this happens, I intentionally stop keying and ask myself: "If I were coaching a group of individuals for bringing out the books inside of them, what words would I use to make my point?" More often than not, this mind game quiets my inner censor and gets me back on the writing track.

Reflection: What are you going to do to control your inner censor rather than letting it control you?

What to Do When Your Writing Engine Sputters

Ink and paper are sometimes passionate lovers, oftentimes brother and sister, and occasionally mortal enemies.

—Terri Guillemets

I would be remiss if I did not tell you that every so often, when I have a scheduled writing appointment with myself, my writing engine sputters. While I don't wish it upon you, I want to prepare you for it because it *will* happen.

You will know what I mean. It will be like turning on the ignition key and not hearing the engine rev. When this happens to me, I do the following in the order listed below:

1. I put on my research hat and go to the iPad that I have dedicated for research to see what else has been written on the topic.

2. I shift from the topic that I was planning to write about and begin writing another section of the book.

3. I reschedule time to write later that day and not a day later. *Let me repeat, not a day later.* Besides rescheduling the time, I also shift my writing zone location in order to start anew.

Reflection: What do you do when you are not revved to make something happen that must get done?

Writing Fitness: How to Stir Up Your Imagination

Imagination will often carry us to worlds that never were. But without it we go nowhere.

—Carl Sagan

Just as your body needs exercise, so does your mind. Getting and keeping your writing muscles in shape, toned, and well rested is essential for stimulating your imagination.

Here are four writing fitness routines that I advocate for keeping your imagination in good shape:

1. Exercise.

Take a walk, go to the gym, swim, or simply stretch. Just move!

2. Make a point of doing something creative.

Go to movies, plays, and musical performances such as chamber music concerts. I find that looking forward to these activities is often as stimulating as attending them.

Doing something creative can also mean playing a game, reading a book, or trying a new recipe. It doesn't matter what you do; what does matter is that you do something *stimulating*. You will see for yourself that when you fire up your neurons by doing something creative, your writing juices will flow.

3. Step away from writing to write.

Yes, you read it right! Step away from your normal writing zone. Choose another writing environment. If you write on the dining room table, go to a spare room to write. If you write in a coffee shop, write on the kitchen table when not a creature is moving, not even a mouse. Eek! We've all had them at one time or another.

4. Take a power nap.

It is amazing what a twenty-minute power nap will do. It totally relaxes your mind. You may not believe your eyes, but I am encouraging you to take a nap as a way of becoming creatively fit. Now if that is not an oxymoron, what is?!

The Japanese have been doing it for years. Based on an *Inc.* article written by Zoe Henry, six US companies that include Uber, Google, Zappos, Capitol One Labs, Ben and Jerry's, and PwC condone power naps.[1] The reason: Power napping actually increases brain power, stamina, alertness, and performance! Do you need more reasons? I sure don't.

Excuse me for thirty minutes. I am off to nap!

Once you figure out what stirs up your imagination, and it will be different along the way, you will be writing with such fluidity that you may feel like your fingers are keying without your help.

Reflection: What writing fitness activities would you use to stir up your imagination?

Why to Stop Writing While You Are Ahead

I averaged writing about four to six hours a day. I quickly learned that if I tried to write any longer, my brain would turn to mush. I would start having to mentally search for words in order to get my point across rather than just letting them flow as my mind spoke to my fingertips.

—Ken Murray, *On Parr*

As an author, your writing voice will become your best friend. Nurture it rather than exploit it by trying to squeeze out one more word from it. Instead, stop while you both still have more to say. I have found this to be a surefire way for your writing voice and you to look forward to your next scheduled get-together even more.

It is the same principle as spending time at a friend's home, yet not overextending your stay by leaving before you run out of things to talk about. It is also like going on vacation just long enough to enjoy it, yet a short enough time that makes you want to return to that vacation spot in the future.

Reflection: Stop writing while you are still ahead. It will allow you to look forward to—rather than dread—your next writing appointment.

How to Control Your Book Deadlines Rather than Letting Them Control You

I love deadlines. I like the whooshing sound they make as they fly by.

—Douglas Adams

I hate people telling me what to do. Anyone in my family will vouch for that.

When I look back on writing my first six books, I realize that I had a love/hate relationship with my manuscripts. Once I got past the euphoric stage of having a publisher accept my book proposals, I felt that I was mentally incarcerated. I knew that I had to cough up the manuscripts by the agreed-upon date in the contract, or else. . . . I never chose to find out what the "or else" could possibly mean short of losing credibility with my publisher.

Then something happened on December 31, 2007. My 2008 New Year's resolution was to consistently arrive early to scheduled gatherings/appointments with family members, friends, and certainly, clients.

Beginning on January 1, 2008, I put this resolution into practice. And it has become part of my life ever since.

(That "anything you do twenty-one times becomes a habit" theory really works.)

To this day, this resolution has remained part of my life. In fact, my family members and friends now call me "too uptight" when it comes to having to arrive places early. You may be asking, why is this so important to me? The reason is that I feel a secret freedom by not being bound by other people's deadlines—say, let's meet at 3:00 p.m.—since I create my own deadline of being early. Oh yes, if you ever invite me to your home, worry not, I will not show up more than two minutes ahead of time.

Soon after putting this resolution into practice, I realized that I would apply the same strategy to the deadlines given to me by my publisher. I began ignoring the requested deadlines and, instead, would make a point of completing book sections earlier than requested.

To this day, I still practice this mental game. Now, meeting those once-dreaded deadlines has taken a back seat. Underpromising and overdelivering has taken precedence.

Here are three other ways to meet deadlines:

1. Plan ahead.

Preschedule writing appointments with yourself and *keep* them. Avoid the dirty word "cancel." If something crucial does come up (life happens!) give yourself a twenty-four-hour cancellation policy and reschedule the time.

2. Stay focused.

Minimize distractions such as any contraption that dings or rings. Turn off the news channel in the background. News is *always* breaking these days, anyway! You won't miss a thing.

3. Put off for tomorrow what is not essential for today.

Note: Meeting your self-imposed deadline is not one of them. And will anyone die if the laundry goes unfolded for another day or the dishes stay in the sink? If so, delegate!

Reflection: What will you do to control your book deadline?

From First Draft to Final Manuscript

It is okay to write garbage—as long as you edit it brilliantly.

—C. J. Cherryh

Many budding authors have asked what it takes to go from writing the first draft of a book to taking it to the final manuscript.

There is no one right answer or length of time for going through this process. With my first eight books, I found rewrites to be rather tedious. So before even beginning to write this book, I decided to be proactive by creating the following six-part system for taking each book section from draft form to the finished manuscript.

1. Write the section.

2. Set the section aside overnight. Note: I had many sleepless nights thinking about how I could explain a topic better.

3. Get up, exercise, and then reread the section. Note: Some of my best modifications came to me when I was sweating.

4. Rewrite the section, if necessary.

5. Send the draft to my three sounding board advisors to critique.

6. Review their recommendations and rewrite the section in its final form.

The two steps that I found most valuable in the process were to step back after writing the first draft and think. The other invaluable step was to have the section critiqued by my sounding board advisors. More often than not, I would interpret their feedback from a reader perspective. Ninety-five percent of the time, their recommendations were integrated into the final manuscript.

I was as interested as you may be to learn how other authors took their writing from draft to finished manuscript form. Here is what they said:

> Since approximately 50 percent of *Get a Grip on Your Grammar* was taken from blogs that were originally on my website, that copy was already edited. The remainder of the manuscript was written less in official drafts and more in a continual tinkering methodology until it felt right. I often do sweeping edits focusing on one emphasis at a time, but this manuscript didn't progress that way. It was tinkered with, sentence by sentence, page by page, until the whole was complete.
> —KRIS SPISAK, AUTHOR, *GET A GRIP ON YOUR GRAMMAR*

> When writing, revision is never done! Every time I looked at it there was something I could add, delete, or change to make it better, clearer, more descriptive. I didn't have multiple drafts per se. I just constantly, constantly, constantly refined. At some point I just decided that parts were finished and finally the whole was finished.
> —LYDIA LAMBERT, AUTHOR,
> *KISSING FROGS: THE PATH TO A PRINCE*

> I only did one initial draft of each chapter but worked on the flow and transitions for about a week. My safety net was that I knew I had at least

two professional editors ready to look it over when I thought it was complete.
—KEN MURRAY, AUTHOR, *ON PARR*

When I was writing *Conscious Ink,* my first draft was my final draft. There was one section in Chapter 3 that started to go off base, so after a few hours of writing, I hit delete and went to the mall. I actually came back inspired and began writing again.

There was also a section in Chapter 5 that took me a few hours to write, and I accidentally deleted it. I could have screamed! In hindsight, it was a blessing in disguise because what I came up with the second time around was much better. Maybe I had some spiritual assistance that caused me to get rid of what I was writing so I could better reframe my content.
—LISA BARRETTA, AUTHOR,
CONSCIOUS INK: THE HIDDEN MEANING OF TATTOOS

Reflection: Before starting to write your book, think through the editing process that will work best for you.

Six Things NOT to Do With Your Manuscript

Maybe you have to know the darkness
before you can appreciate the light.

—Madeleine L'Engle

As you may remember from the section "How Long Does It Take to Write a Book?," you will invest hundreds of hours of your precious time writing your manuscript depending on the number of words you write per hour and the length of your book. If you choose to write your masterpiece in longhand, it will even take longer.

Yes, you read it right *longhand*. You may be as surprised as I was to discover how many authors forgo using a tech tool and instead put pen to paper. If you don't believe me, go to Yohana Desta's February 15, 2014, article on *Mashable.com*. In her piece, "10 Famous Writers Who Don't Use Modern Tech to Create,"[1] you will discover that Quentin Tarantino, George R. R. Martin, Joyce Carol Oates, Neil Gaiman, Amy Tan, Tom Wolfe, George Clooney, Jhumpa Lahiri, and P. J. O'Rourke put pen to paper when writing their manuscripts. Since most people are creatures of habit, you also will discover that Danielle Steel continues to write her books on a 1946 Olympia manual typewriter.

So, whether you choose to use a tech tool, typewriter, or write your book in longhand, plan ahead by having a system to back up your work. You may think that losing what you have written will never happen to you. If/when it does, you will have wished you would have taken this advice.

Not convinced? Here are six manuscript scenarios that you can easily avoid:

1. You keep your only draft within reach of your canine.

Toby, John Steinbeck's Irish Setter, shredded the only draft *Of Mice and Men,* which accounted for two month's work.[2] If this happened to you, would you be a mouse by swearing off rewriting the book or a man like Steinbeck and rewrite it? I bet Toby's days were numbered.

2. You give the one and only book manuscript to an angry spouse.

Robert Louis Stevenson's wife, Fanny, burned the first draft of *Jekyll and Hyde*—one of the world's most admired and profound horror stories—after dismissing it to a friend as "a quire full of utter nonsense."[3] Stevenson spent the next three days rewriting and redrafting the 30,000-word story by hand.

3. You give family members easy access to your manuscript.

In December 1922, Hadley, Ernest Hemingway's wife, thought she was doing her husband a favor. She packed his unfinished manuscripts to take to Switzerland where they were to meet Lincoln Steffens, an American reporter. When she stepped away from the suitcase for a moment, it vanished—as did Hemingway's work.[4]

4. You store your only manuscript in a location that is not waterproof.

As many as seven of Stephen King's original typed manuscripts, including *Dolan's Cadillac, Maximum Overdrive,* and *The Eyes of the Dragon* were believed to be ruined after a pipe flooded the basement of several downtown Bangor businesses.[5] Luckily, these early works had already been published.

5. You give the only copy of your manuscript to someone for review.

Thomas Carlyle, author of *The French Revolution,* loaned the original draft of this work to his friend John Stuart Mill for comment. Mill told him a maid had mistaken it for waste paper and burned it. Carlyle had to rewrite it from scratch.[6]

6. You forget where you put the only copy of your manuscript.

James Michener set aside more than half of his original manuscript of the novel *Mexico.* He found his narrative thirty years later after a relative discovered it stashed away in two cardboard boxes.[7] Ginkgo, anyone?

I hope that these scenarios have reinforced the importance of backing up your manuscript. The last thing you want is to lose your labor of love.

The reason that this topic is so near and dear to my heart is three years ago, I lost fifteen hours of writing for one careless reason: I had not backed up my work. If I had my tech devices downloaded to the Cloud, saved my work on a USB or hard drive, or merely emailed it to a friend, this dilemma would not have happened.

Confession time: You're probably not going to believe this, but I had to rewrite *this very section* for one reason: I did not take my own advice to back it up!

Reflection: How are you going to consistently back up your book manuscript?

Your Name or a Pen Name?

A pen name is a nickname.

—A. D. Posey

When you decide to bring out the book in you, are you going to use your name or a pseudonym? I never gave a second thought to using a fictitious name when writing. The thought of using a pen name, however, is becoming more intriguing with each word being keyed. If I were to write the book about my days of dating guys of every star sign, a pseudonym might be in order.

So why do authors use a pen name in the first place? There are an infinite number of reasons. Let me give you four of them:

1. When writing about a topic in which readers might question their expertise based on gender.

For example, what if you flipped through a book called *A Smart Woman's Survival Guide for Motherhood Through Menopause* and noticed that it was written by a man? Unless he was among the top one percent of the most hyper-intuitive men roaming the planet *and* a gynecological MD, you would likely question how he could authentically know about how to survive such ordeals.

If the same male author, however, wrote the book and used a female pen name, it is doubtful that you or I would—at least at first—question this person's survival methods and her eagerness to share them with the world. Likewise, if you saw a guidebook entitled *Finding the Perfect Football Helmet*, you would probably be more prone to trust its advice if a male athlete authored it. Of course, I'm not suggesting that females don't play mean football and know how to protect their skulls with proper gear, and that males cannot truly relate to hormonal imbalances and impossible life disruptions, just that you as the writer have the option to choose a pen name that audiences would more likely trust at first glance.

2. Another writing voice in you is speaking.

A well-known mystery writer needs a break from writing in a genre that he is known for. He has found another writing voice—one that is compelling him to write a cookbook. He is concerned that his fan-base may be disappointed by his about turn of topics.

By using a pseudonym, this author can easily deviate from his readers' expectations of mysterious twists and turns. He can simply hide behind his pen name and write *25 Ways to Prepare an Egg Without Breaking the Yoke*.

3. You have a ubiquitous name.

An author has a John Doe name. Rather than risking that readers will confuse his book with authors of the same name, he proactively creates a unique pen name.

4. You are coauthoring a book, yet prefer it to look like it has been written by one author.

This is what two sisters, Valerie and Lynne Constantine, did. They chose to work in collaboration by creating Liv Constantine as their pen name. It worked for them, and their thrilling murder mysteries became international bestsellers.

Now, before you jump gung ho into using a pen name, consider the two disadvantages:

1. You remain anonymous. In other words, you are ghostwriting your own story.

2. You need to be mindful of maintaining your pseudonym identity when representing your book.

3. You should seek the counsel of a tax attorney who will assist you in taking the appropriate legal steps for using a pen name.[1]

Now let's get the juice firsthand from the author of *Kissing Frogs: The Path to a Prince* who has been using the pen name of Lydia Lambert since 2005:

What prompted you to write under a pseudonym?

At the time I finished *Kissing Frogs,* I had a son in college, and I wasn't sure how he would handle the subject of his mom's dating escapades. In addition, I was running for school board, and I wasn't sure if my dating profile was electable. Even though it was "my story," I did not want to publicize that part of my life. It still didn't mesh with the life I was living.

How did individuals in your personal and professional life react when they discovered that you were the author of *Kissing Frogs: The Path to a Prince?*

Reactions to the book were mixed. Some made snide comments about it. Still others tried to figure out who was who. Some people, even those close to me, still don't know that I've written a book.

How did you introduce yourself at book signings?

I did address myself as Lydia Lambert at book signings and more recently at the pitch fest.

How did you create the name "Lydia Lambert"?

Once at a happy hour with friends, early in my single life, we decided to come up with a name in case guys wanted to pick us up—ready responses that weren't our real names.

I picked "Lydia" because it started with *L* (I wear a lot of monogrammed jewelry) and it had three syllables—the same as my legal name. I chose "Lambert" because it was the name of one of my friends in elementary school.

Would you like to know who Lydia Lambert really is? I'll never tell!

While authors who use pen names may be seen as having a certain mystique, they often use pseudonyms for practical reasons. For example, one author uses Erica Kirov when publishing for young readers because she doesn't want these readers to pick up any of her adult titles.

Here is why she made the decision to use a pen name:

Prior to the release of the first book in my middle-grade series, The Magickeepers, I was also the author of some edgier romantic comedies, as well as an extremely dark noir novel. My publisher and I decided a pen name would enable me to keep those two writing personas separate. After the first Magickeepers book came out, I was frequently doing school appearances—and so for a while I maintained separate websites and was careful to only use my pen name in front of kids.

I think today it's a little harder because kids are so tech savvy, and in the era of social media, etc., it's trickier to keep a pen name "secret." Still, it lets readers know what kind of book to expect.

Reflection: If you choose to use a pen name, what would be your motivation? What pseudonym would you choose?

Ghostwriting: Bringing a Book Out In Someone Else

Because you happen to be a writer doesn't mean you have to deny yourself the ordinary human pleasure of being praised and applauded.

—Philip Roth, *The Ghost Writer*

Now that you have gotten this far in *Everybody Has a Book Inside of Them,* you may be a few steps closer to bringing out that book inside of you. Or are you? If you *are* chomping at the bit to start writing a book, yet not your own, perhaps ghostwriting may be the next step for you.

Now, before you even consider hanging out your ghostwriting shingle to let other would-be authors in the world know that you are ready to become *their* voice, see if these four descriptions fit you:

1. You love writing—plain and simple.
2. You like anonymity.
3. You do not want the responsibility of book promotion.
4. Although you may not have written your own book yet, you have excellent credentials as a professional writer or journalist.

If you are still enticed by the thought of bringing out a book in someone else, I would like you to hear firsthand what a ghostwriter has to say about this process. In addition to authoring her own book, Kris Spisak *(https://Kris-Spisak. com/ghostwriting/)* has ghostwritten four nonfiction books to date, including subjects from personal development to business strategy for niche industries to a memoir that she wrote in the style of a thriller—which she shared was a lot of fun.

Here are Kris Spisak's seven ghostwriting tips:

1. Capture the voice of the person you are ghosting.

Make sure the book you are ghostwriting never sounds like you. It should always sound like the named author of the book.

2. Listen to your client's speech patterns and style.

This should be included in your "author brand" brainstorming. Spend time talking a lot with your client so you can listen to and become familiar with his or her speech patterns and style. This detail alone separates professional ghostwriters from those who might just be starting out. Voice can be challenging, and getting it right isn't easy. But getting it right is an essential piece of the process.

3. Know your role.

Always remember that a ghostwriter is a silent partner in the project after its published, but in the creative process, *you* are the one in the driver's seat. It's a bit of an adventure to take someone else's concepts and flesh them out into an entire book. Enjoy the process of stretching your creative muscles along the way.

4. The client is almost always right.

The hardest part is to remember that the project is not 100 percent your own. You should have discussions about why you're making certain choices for the sake of the project as a whole, and oftentimes, your industry and craft expertise will win out over an initial impulse that wouldn't be the right choice. However, on occasion your client will hold firm on something you disagree with. As they are the client, you need to handle their project as they'd like.

5. Retrieving the content will vary based on each client.

You will find some clients prefer weekly face-to-face interview chats while others may give you a rough (really, really rough, sometimes) draft. They may even tell you to rewrite it in a certain style. Other clients may feel more comfortable sending you a collection of voice memos whenever ideas strike them, rather than written notes. Retrieving the content depends on the comfort level of each unique client, but one way or another, you will always find a way to get there.

6. Ask the right questions.

Consider yourself a coach in the content-gathering phase. Begin with themes. Ask yourself what the big ideas are of the project that your client—the visible author—wants to ensure will be in the book. Ask yourself what the reader takeaways should be. What moments are the momentous scenes of the story? When those are solidified (often after many conversations), create a shared file on each subject and start filling up each of these buckets with content.

7. Gain credibility as a ghostwriter.

Build your portfolio. No one will be interested in hiring you if you don't have any endorsements or others who can recommend you as a talented wordsmith.

Read widely. If an author—your client—wants a memoir in the style of *Eat, Pray, Love*, a motivational book that might be enjoyed by readers of Brené Brown, or a business book that goes through a strategy point by point like *The 7*

Habits of Highly Effective People, you need to know what that means.

Continue to work on your craft. No matter whether you're writing a book with your own name on the cover or not, writing can be hard. The more you write and the more you practice editing, the better you become. If you continue to dedicate yourself to bettering your craft, it will show in your work, and thus, more clients will follow.

Although it is not a requirement to be a published author to be a ghostwriter, a strong track record in writing and editing are essential. That experience may be in corporate storytelling or in book editing before taking the leap into ghostwriting.

Your experience in writing a full-length book is mandatory. While that doesn't have to be formal training, familiarity with the structure of the genre you're working in makes all the difference.

Reflection: When you are ready to write a book, do you foresee preferring to bring out the book inside of you or to ghostwrite a book for someone else?

The Five "If You Were to Write A Book" Questions to Ask Before Beginning to Write

Fill your paper with the breathings of your heart.

—William Wordsworth

I remember presenting a sales-training program for an unseasoned group of wealth management advisors. Many of these individuals had finance backgrounds. Like most individuals in the professional services industry, the last thing that they wanted to be labeled as was (God forbid) *salespeople*.

I assured them that in order to be successful, they would *never* have to do the dirty work of "selling." What they would need to do, I went on to tell them, was to get people to *buy*. And the way to make this buying process happen was to ask their potential clients the following three "If you were" questions:

1. If you were able to change one thing about your existing investment advisor's strategies for your portfolio, what would it be?

2. If you were to invest your existing cash, what would your risk tolerance be?

3. If you were ready to invest additional money, how much do you have to invest?

So now it is your turn. Let me ask you five "If you were" questions. (You get more questions because you are special.)

1. If you were to start writing, what would be your chosen genre?

If you enjoy cooking, perhaps the genre would be food and wine. If you love the world of finance, the book inside of you might be a book on business and money. If you are fascinated by people's lives, you might choose to write a biography or memoir.

2. If you were to start writing the book inside of you, who would be your readers?

Who would be your audience? Keep in mind that before your fingers touch that keyboard, it is imperative that you know your reader. This will help you develop the writing style that will be of most interest to them for communicating your message.

Think about it. You tailor your email messages and texts to the individuals who are receiving them. The way you write—your style and content—should be based on the persons for whom you are writing or for whom you want to attract.

3. If you were to start writing, which days and at what time of day would you schedule time to write?

Just as you schedule appointments with others, it is essential to schedule a writing appointment with yourself on a consistent basis. If you can schedule time to write daily—

even for only thirty minutes—do so. You will be doing yourself a favor by creating a new habit.

Note: Anything you do twenty-one times becomes a habit.

Let me tell you about the writing appointments that I made with myself when writing my last book as well as with the one you are in the midst of reading:

When writing *What Self-Made Millionaires Do That Most People Don't*, I had four months to complete the manuscript. Since I did not want this project to take time from my workday, I created time to write during "off hours."

Beginning September 1, 2017, through December 31, 2017, I went to bed at 10:00 p.m., and then woke up at 2:30 a.m. With a cup of coffee in hand, I would write for an hour and a half to two hours, then go back to bed until 7:00 a.m. or 8:00 a.m. (Coffee does not affect my sleep.) While that may sound like masochistic behavior to you, it worked well for me. The reason: At that time of the morning, I could hear my inner voice speak, which allowed me to write without the distraction of neither human nor canine making a peep.

On the other hand, when writing *Everybody Has a Book Inside of Them: How to Bring It Out,* my scheduled session times were totally different. What worked for me with this manuscript was to begin writing from 10:00 p.m. to 11:30 p.m. and again for an hour and a half with that first cup of morning coffee. When I traveled for business, my morning scheduled writing sessions were in-flight.

My reason for sharing this info with you is to reinforce that there is not a "right time" to write. The bewitching hours for you will be the ones that work best based on what is going on in the rest your life.

4. When do you envision scheduling your writing appointments?

If the thought is crossing your mind that you don't have the time to write, then you are not ready to begin your book. There was a ten-year gap between writing my eighth book, *One Minute Manners,* and my ninth book, *What Self-Made Millionaires Do That Most People Don't.* I had no interest in writing another book during that decade. Life got in the way. You will know when it is time to bring out the book in you. When the timing and topic are right, you will be willing to make writing a priority.

Only begin writing your book when you are ready. Listen to your writing voice rather than anyone else guilting you into starting your book. Otherwise, you will resent both the person and the project. Writing the book inside of you is too magical an experience to dread doing it.

I will promise you, dear reader, that when your time is right to begin writing the book inside of you, you will add a dimension to your life that you have yet to experience.

5. If you were to start writing, who would be the one or two people you would choose to be your sounding boards?

Your chosen sounding boards should be comprised of two to three individuals whose opinions you value. Choose people who will be candid about your book's content. Encourage them to make writing modifications after reading your manuscript. When selecting this advisory sounding board, be sure that these individuals represent your readership audience.

When receiving constructive criticism from these individuals, take their advice professionally rather than personally. By doing so, they will feel more comfortable about being candid. And while you, of course, have the final say about how you want your book to read, set your ego aside when recommendations are made. Remind yourself that your sounding board advisors are on your side. They too want to assist you in making your book the best that it can be.

Reflection: Give serious thought to your answers for the five questions. They will be instrumental in setting the stage for your writing journey.

What Are You Waiting For? Start Writing Now!

The scariest moment is always just before you start.
—Stephen King

The time to bring out the book inside of you is now. If you don't believe me, you will by the time you finish reading this section.

Wouldn't it be terrible to be on your deathbed with all your mental faculties and know there was a book inside of you that you did not bring out?

Although I want you to have a good taste in your mouth by the time you finish this book, I also want to give you a reality check. Your clock is ticking, so begin listening to your writing voice and start keying.

When I say that everybody has a book inside of them, I mean it. I must admit, however, that those words were more powerful than I even realized.

Let me give you a case in point example: When I was in the middle of writing this book, I went into my partner's home office to surprise him with a good morning kiss and I ended up being the one who was surprised! He was sitting at his desk with his laptop in front of him. His fingers were touching his keyboard and it was not an email that he was sending.

When I leaned down to give him that kiss, I was thrilled and admittedly stunned to see that *he* had started writing the manuscript that he teasingly talked about yet swore he would never write: his book of jokes.

When I congratulated him on bringing out the book in *him*, I asked how he did it. He replied, "You kept hounding me, so I started by keying one word, then one sentence, then one paragraph. Before I knew it, I wrote one page, and now a section is finished."

It was obvious. This master violinist was letting his inner voice speak through his fingers unto the keyboard with the same fluidity that his fingers travel on his violin's fingerboard. Allan is bringing out the book inside of him. So can you.

If you need more convincing, read on to hear the powerful message below by Barbara Mitchell, author of *The Big HR Handbook:*

> Don't wait until you have time or the perfect moment—it doesn't exist—just get started and see where it takes you.

Now, if Barbara Mitchell's words or mine have not struck your writing nerve, then read on for Lydia Lambert's (no, I am still *not* going to tell you her real name) advice, author of *Kissing Frogs: The Path to a Prince:*

> My father was a writer, and he appreciated my talent for writing and had always said that he and I should cowrite a book. My father died in 2000, and I was struck by the fact that we had never achieved that dream of writing a book. So part of my drive was the need to take care of unfinished business and get my story out and on the shelf.

You must be heading to your keyboard by now. If you are not and need more convincing, then here is one last reality check from author Ken Murray, who wrote *On Parr:*

I had always had a thought that someday in my post–Air Force life, I'd sit down with my father, who was a forty-nine-year editor of a small-town newspaper in Iowa featuring his weekly column How I See It by Cliff Murray. I thought that would be a great way to get him to come stay with us in Texas to escape the cold and harsh Iowa winter months. This would enable us to put pen to paper or fingers to keyboards to regurgitate his weekly thoughts from his columns over the years. Our goal: to meld his previous writings and his current-day "senior" thought processes that inevitably would vector readers to tears during one chapter then bursting out into a full belly laugh in another. All those plans were dashed when he passed away the day after I retired from the Air Force in 2011.

Please email me at *annmarie@bringoutyourbook.com* when you begin to bring out that book in you. I will not take no for an answer. And *please,* do not use having too little time as an excuse. We all have the same twenty-four hours. It is how we choose to use them.

Reflection: What is it going to take to bring out the book in you?

What to Include in Your Writing Pledge of Allegiance

Unless commitment is made, there are only promises and hopes; but no plans.

—Peter F. Drucker

If you have gotten this far in *Everybody Has a Book Inside of Them*, then I would venture to say that you are several steps closer to bringing out that book in you than where you were when you started reading.

While the timeline for writing your book is up to you, I felt like it was up to me, dear reader, to prepare you for your writing journey. Even though this is my tenth book, I willingly admit that, as I was writing many of the sections I felt very vulnerable sharing my deep, dark writing preparation secrets with you. It will have been worth feeling exposed, however, if my secrets help to bring out the book in you.

When you are ready to begin your writing journey, I encourage you to complete the following Writing Pledge of Allegiance. It is for you and no one else to see. It will hold you accountable—to yourself, that is—for taking the first step to make your book a reality. Please know that I am only one keystroke away for you.

Happy writing!

Writing Pledge of Allegiance

1. I will write a minimum of _____ words a day.

2. I will write for a minimum of _____ hours a day, _____ days a week.

3. I will give myself _____ (name the day of the week) as my day off.

4. I have identified _____ (name the locations) where I will go into my writing zones.

5. I will ask _____ (name one to three people) to be my writing sounding boards. I will ask them to keep what I send to them confidential.

6. I will take constructive criticism from my chosen sounding board buddies professionally rather than personally.

7. In order to stay both mentally and physically healthy during this rigorous writing process, I will nourish my body and mind by exercising a minimum of _____ hours a week as well as by eating healthy.

8. I will make a point of doing one creative activity a week in order to stay mentally stimulated.

9. My book manuscript will be finished by _____ (list a specific date).

10. I will celebrate my book's completion by giving myself _____ (list a specific gift).

Reflection: You keep your word with others. Take your Writing Pledge of Allegiance, and be sure to keep your word to yourself.

Why the "How to Get Published" Section Is Not Being Addressed in This Book

If Moses were alive today, he'd come down from the mountain with the Ten Commandments and spend the next five years trying to get them published.

—Anonymous

Asking about the publishing route to take before actually writing your book is like asking, "Which came first, the chicken or the egg?" It is like telling a newly married couple about all of the sleepless nights they will have with their newborn rather than allowing them to savor the joy of creating a child.

If a budding author like you and expectant couples knew what was ahead of them, neither might ever move forward. So rather than, as they say, "biting off more than you can chew," I have one request: Focus on bringing out the book inside of you.

Please know that I will be discussing in length what it takes to get published—with 100 percent certainty. I will be with you the entire way as you go through the process of getting published in my eleventh book, *How to*

Get Your Book Published and Sell It as Though Your Life Depends On It.

So for now, savor the fact that you have a book inside of you. I am telling you how to bring it out, so get going!

Oh, by the way, I can read minds. Has the thought crossed your mind, "Why should I expend my energy writing a book when I may never get a book publishing contract?" Aha! I told you I could read your mind! If that is what you are thinking, then do two things for me, and most importantly, for yourself:

1. Go back and reread the section "How Authors Dispel Those Dirty Writing Doubts from Their Minds." Then start writing down your doubts and shredding them until they are gone.

2. Keep the faith! Don't worry about spinning your wheels in vain. I am *not* going to let you do that to yourself. You can always self-publish! So, you are and will remain in your book-writing driver's seat. As I said before and I will repeat, get going!

Reflection: First things first! Rather than worry about getting your book published, start by identifying the book inside of you. Next, give yourself an attainable deadline. Finally, find a loving someone who will give you a KITA to start writing!

Answers to Questions You May Not Have Thought to Ask!

How Soon Is Too Soon to Write Your Second Book After Writing Your First?

Keep a small can of WD-40 on your desk—away from open flames—to remind yourself that if you don't write daily, you will get rusty.

—George Singleton

The chapter title question is like asking, "How soon should you conceive your second child after having your first?" Sometimes you have no choice: it just happens!

You may wonder why I included this section when you may not have even brought out the first book in you. The reason: to prepare you if your writing voice unexpectedly takes over.

There is no hard-and-fast rule to follow for starting your second book after finishing your first one. You will not believe your eyes when you read that some authors actually write two to four books simultaneously. Perhaps they are the same people who read more than one book at a time. While I can multitask pretty well, personally, I cannot imagine reading, or for that matter, writing more than one book at a time.

If you can see yourself as a juggler of writing multiple books, then recognize that it has been successfully done. If you wonder why anyone in their right mind would take on this task, here are the possible reasons:

1. Writing multiple books simultaneously is stimulating.

2. They are under multiple book contracts with close deadlines.

If writing multiple books at the same time floats your boat, then go for it. If you think that writing multiple books is total lunacy, then avoid putting yourself in that situation.

During my twenty-seven years of authoring books, there have been a range of six months to ten years between finishing one manuscript before beginning another. After writing my eighth book, I swore I was finished birthing books. Never say never!

Ten years after saying "never," my writing bug returned. I was not sure that I wanted to dedicate the time to writing another book, yet continued to be haunted until once again, I let my writing voice rule. That is how *What Self-Made Millionaires Do That Most People Don't* came about!

So as you see, the right time to write your second book is when you hear your inner voice speak to you. Take it from me. Do not try to quiet it. If your writing voice is anything like mine, it will only speak louder until your fingers start to key.

Reflection: Consider whether you are the type of writer who would have just one book in process or several at once. Would you feel more inspired or completely overwhelmed by the idea of your next writing project peeking out its head while you are still on your first?

Do Authors Write More than One Book at a Time?

A book is really like a lover. It arranges itself in your life in a way that is beautiful.

—Maurice Sendak

Just as some people can multitask, some authors write more than one book at a time. That was a new fact for me until my Uber trip from a hotel in Plano, Texas, to the Dallas/ Ft. Worth International Airport in October 2018.

Although it was only 4:30 a.m., I struck up a conversation with the driver who happened to be a rather distinguished gentleman. He had been born and raised in Johannesburg. His late wife had been an agent for several famous actors whom you and I have seen on the movie screen. And this retired gent had spent his career writing several historical fiction romances.

You must be thinking that I am as gullible as they come; however, I know it for a fact because I looked up his books on Amazon the minute he told me—in the dark and all—and there he was!

When this Uber driver gentleman got my suitcase out of his trunk and handed it to me, I extended my hand to thank him for telling me his story. He took my hand and kissed it, making me feel as though we were the characters in one of his historical fiction novels—the one with a little romance.

Back to the topic: While the trip was not long enough for me to ask him how he juggled writing more than one book at a time, I did ask my two Career Press author colleagues how they did it.

Here is what Marie D. Jones and Gail Z. Martin said:

I tend to write one nonfiction book, one novel, and one script all at the same time. It just works for me because it allows me to step away from one and go to the other, and going back and forth keeps my ideas flowing and my motivation up.

I never get stuck or get writer's block. There are times when I am writing two different nonfiction books or two novels or two screenplays, and I usually make sure they are not the same genre, so I don't end up using the same voice and ideas for both!
—MARIE D. JONES, AUTHOR, *BLACK WOLF, WHITE SWAN*

I'm constantly switching among genres, which also means changing up time periods, geographic locations (in the books), and character worldview. I try to bring out new books in each series on a regular basis, so that means moving seamlessly from one project to the next and alternating series. Never a dull moment!
—GAIL Z. MARTIN, AUTHOR,
THE ESSENTIAL SOCIAL MEDIA MARKETING HANDBOOK AND
30 DAYS TO SOCIAL MEDIA SUCCESS

Reflection: If by now you can see yourself actually bringing out the book that is inside of you, can you imagine yourself birthing two books at the same time?

What Makes Authors Write in More than One Genre?

Don't classify me, read me. I'm a writer, not a genre.

—Carlos Fuentes

Writing in more than one genre is more common than you think. In fact, in an November 2, 2017, article for *Bustle*, Sadie Trombetta states that thirteen bestselling authors write in more than one genre.[1] These authors include J. K. Rowling, Isabel Allende, Stephen King, and Neil Gaiman.

For example, J. K. Rowling, best known for the Harry Potter children's fantasy book series, took a book genre detour in 2012. She wrote her first adult novel, *The Casual Vacancy*. Then in 2013, J. K. Rowling received praise from other crime writers when she joined them in this genre by authoring *The Cuckoo's Calling* under the pseudonym of Robert Galbraith.

Two other prolific authors whom you heard from throughout this book explained why they choose to write in more than one genre.

> Rather than get stuck writing in just one genre, I made sure to do a book in between that was different and broke me out of any mold. Although the majority of my books can be put into a niche, I have written a

handful that cannot and they have allowed me to be diverse in writing anything I like.

—MARIE D. JONES, AUTHOR, *EKHO: EVIL KID HUNTING ORGANIZATION*

I gain a broader audience because I can offer books for a variety of reader tastes. If you aren't into one genre, you may like another. It also keeps me fresh because the conventions of each genre are very different, as are the voice, writing style, vocabulary, etc. It keeps me on my toes!

—GAIL Z. MARTIN, AUTHOR, *THE ESSENTIAL SOCIAL MEDIA MARKETING HANDBOOK* AND *30 DAYS TO SOCIAL MEDIA SUCCESS*

How Gail Z. Martin began writing nonfiction:

For nonfiction, the books flowed from what I found myself answering the most questions about when I was doing a lot of marketing consulting. People wanted to know how to use social media strategically and how to create a consistent brand, as well as how to fine-tune social media for specific industries (speakers, small business, authors, nonprofit, etc.). One book, *Fresh Start Success,* arose out of knowing so many people who had made successful life and career changes and that there were so many more who wanted to make those same kinds of changes but were held back by fear.

Why Gail Z. Martin began writing fiction:

For fiction, it's really been a matter of the heart. Epic fantasy was my first love, and I now have four different epic fantasy series, with a fifth one starting this year. Then I fell in love with urban fantasy, and I now write or cowrite three urban fantasy series. We wanted to explore paranormal historical/steampunk, so that kicked off another series.

And then I fell in love with urban fantasy/MM/paranormal romance, and so (as Morgan Brice) I now have two series out in that genre.

Reflection: Can you picture yourself writing in more than one genre?

Does Your Writing Voice Change When You Write in Different Genres?

Writing is the painting of the voice.

—Voltaire

The answer is yes. Just as you can make your speaking voice softer, louder, higher, and lower, your writing voice will also change based on the genre you choose.

You may not have even written your first book, yet I am talking to you about writing in different genres. Now don't let me scare you off. I have included this topic so that you know when you decide on the genre for your first book, you will not be bound by that genre for future books.

Keep reading, and you will see what I mean.

Marie D. Jones, author, *The Disaster Survive Guide: How to Prepare for and Survive Floods, Fires, Earthquakes, and More* writes in three different formats: fiction, nonfiction, and film/television. She has written more than twenty books in twelve different genres. Seven of them have been in fiction to include sci-fi, thriller, comedy, drama, horror, satire, adventure for fiction, paranormal, metaphysics, self-help, science, and current events. She is the first to admit that she has different writing voices.

My nonfiction voice helps me to make sure I am conveying my ideas and research clearly and in a way that is enjoyable and easy to digest. I have a writing style that has taken me a while to develop and I am known for it. I can take very complex ideas and simplify them, even including humor and personal experience to get my points across.

When writing fiction, I have a creative voice that is my own, and I have another voice or style when writing screenplays. Yet I believe that in all those arenas, I have a singularly identifiable style. I am not sure how to describe it, but people who read my work tell me they can tell it is me.

—Marie D. Jones, author,
The Disaster Survive Guide: How to Prepare for and Survive Floods, Fires, Earthquakes, and More

I asked Gail Z. Martin, author of seventy-six books, how she developed her different writing voices for her fantasy and fiction books and her business and money books. Here is what she said:

That's never been difficult for me. It's like the difference between speaking to friends and family, and stepping into playing a role in a theater production. I get very distinct "voices" for my characters in my mind, in terms of word choice, diction, speaking style, etc. That also varies by time period (I'm constantly checking to see if words or phrases were in use at different periods in history to avoid anachronisms). Even in the urban fantasy series, which all exist in the same time period (and whose characters cross over and interact with each other), the voices and personalities have to remain distinct so readers can tell who's who. That's especially important when the books are produced as audiobooks and listeners can't just check to see who's talking.

For nonfiction, my voice is more conversational, although still different from a transcript of presentations I've given. I try to make the nonfiction very down-to-earth, easy to understand, easy to put into action. Like having a discussion with a friend.

The fiction voice varies depending on the series and genre. I write epic fantasy, urban fantasy, steampunk, comedic horror, and paranormal romance. The voice in each not only varies by the expectations for how a book in that particular genre should sound, but also by the personalities of the characters. Some are snarky, some are serious, some are over the top. That's one of the best parts of writing, because there's never a dull moment!

—GAIL Z. MARTIN, AUTHOR,
THE ESSENTIAL SOCIAL MEDIA MARKETING HANDBOOK AND
30 DAYS TO SOCIAL MEDIA SUCCESS

Reflection: Listen to how your voice changes based on different situations. This is how your writing voice may change based on your book genre.

What Are the Benefits of Writing in More than One Genre?

That's something I want to do: cover all sorts of genres to find the one I love the most.

—Ella Purnell

Could writing in more than one genre be like speaking more than one language? One way to find out is by asking authors who have done so. Here is what two of them said:

> Working in different genres allows me more freedom to write what I want and not be stuck in one niche or box. I like to write everything and to be able to jump from horror to comedy, screenplay to novel.

While it works for Marie, she encourages budding authors to find their own voices and genres that work best for them.

Here is why Gail Z. Martin has chosen to write in different genres:

> Interestingly enough, I'm frequently tapped to speak on social media at genre conventions because the event organizers know I've written books on the subject and practice what I preach. I've spoken at some of the largest genre conventions in the United States on social media, so there's crossover between

my fiction and nonfiction audiences. And on a lesser note, there have been a fair number of readers who found my nonfiction or knew me as a speaker/consultant, found out about my fiction, and became fans!

Reflection: What do you see as the benefit(s) of writing in more than one genre?

Fourteen Budding Author FAQs

A single conversation across the table with a wise man is better than ten years mere study of books.

—Henry Wadsworth Longfellow

Before writing a book, is it a good idea to review other books that have been written on my intended subject?

Definitely. That is one of the activities in which I partake during my thirty-day incubation period before allowing myself to write. I visit *Amazon.com* to see who has written what on the subject that I am about to write. I look at their content, their book structure, and how they put their personalities into their books. I then analyze what will make my book different from theirs and figure out what I can do to make my book different.

In the section "The Value of a Sounding Board Advisory Group," you shared how important the feedback from these individuals was to you. Apart from these chosen advisors, do you recommend sharing with others that you are writing a book?

When I decide to write a book, I am very discriminating about with whom I share my project. I treat it the same way many couples do when they find out they are expecting.

Other than announcing the news to family and a few close friends, I wait to announce it for at least three months. The reason: I want to have a handle on what I am writing and often only tell others when I would like their feedback about the book topic.

I can say for certain that other than my sounding board advisors, my children, and the person(s) whom I have asked to endorse the book, no one gets a sneak preview of the manuscript until it is published.

When writing, how do you keep from getting distracted?

Since hearing a pin drop distracts me, I often go to bed by 10:00 p.m. and then get up at 4:00 a.m. to write. You'll be surprised how much you can write in two hours without interruption. When I write during the day, I wear earbuds or headphones. It helps me to better tune in to my inner writing voice.

How do I overcome the feeling that I don't write well enough to author a book?

I have only one thing to say to you. Get over it! If you continue to tell yourself that you do not write well enough to join the author ranks, you will eventually talk yourself into not doing it.

Instead, I want you to create a positive mindset. Recognize that you are the sum of the four people with whom you spend the most time. Begin living your author-in-the-making dream by joining a writers' group in your area. Listen to author-in-the-making podcasts, webinars, and blogs. Reread this book and start making it happen.

I have told you what it took for me to write my ten books and so have fifteen other authors. You can do it; you just have to want it. If you need an extra boost, email me at *annmarie@bringoutyourbook.com.* I will give you a KITA!

When writing each of your ten books, did you ever want to quit?

Did you say "quit"? That dirty word is not in my vocabulary. Neither should it be in yours.

I live by two mottos: "Start what you finish" and "Keep your word." Did I ever step away from my manuscript? Yes. Quit? Not on your life!

There were days, I will admit, when my inner writing voice and I needed a break from each other. I would give it a rest and it would leave me alone for the time being. I would use the writing allotted time that day to do research. Other days when my inner writing voice and I were not in sync, I would dedicate my prescheduled writing time to simply *think*. It became a great way to refuel my writing engine.

If you have the term "quit" (ouch, it even hurts to write it) in your vocabulary, assign a writing buddy to be your accountability partner. That person's responsibility will be to cheer you on when those dirty writing doubts creep into your mind.

Besides being cheered on by your accountability partner when the thought of quitting even crosses your mind, schedule a meeting with yourself: Remind yourself why you chose to write your book in the first place. Tell yourself who will benefit from it and how you would be doing a disservice to both potential readers and yourself by not finishing what you started.

Tell yourself that the easy way out would be to quit. Write down why you feel that way. Then wrap up your pity party and schedule your next writing session.

Will anyone read what I write?

That is like asking, "Will your child be admitted to XYZ private school?" when your child hasn't even been born. Write an informative and entertaining book, and people will indeed read what you write. Second-guessing yourself is a waste of time, so get down to business.

When writing my book, do you suggest that I use a laptop, iPad, or paper and pen to write it?

The way you document your thoughts is totally up to you. I strongly encourage you, however, to follow the three steps below:

1. Dedicate one writing tool of choice exclusively for your book.

2. Make sure this tool is not connected to the Internet.

3. Have a tech tool near you from which you can connect to the Internet for research purposes.

Is there a psychology behind the writing tools that authors use to write?

Definitely. People subconsciously choose specific writing tools that enhance their creative energy. Whether or not they realize it, it is based on neurolinguistics, or simply put, the way their neurons are connected.

Approximately 75 percent of writers are **visual**. These individuals choose monitors and keyboards, laptops, or iPads as their writing resources. When surveying friends and family members ages twenty-five to eighty who are visual, I was surprised to learn that some of them also preferred a notebook and pen/pencil as their writing choice.

If you are a **sensory** or **hands-on** person like approximately 15 percent of the world population, you also may use a keyboard. I am this type of person and love writing on my iPad without a keyboard. Other kinesthetic authors who I know use their laptops or monitors with keyboards. The tactile experience is important for *feeling* creatures like us.

The last 10 percent of individuals are **auditory**. My partner, who is a violinist, and an acupuncturist friend are both this type. When asked how they would transmit their thoughts for writing a book, they both said they would use some type of talk-to-text dictation software.

So, you see, the right tool is the one that works best for you. Choosing the one that fits you is essential for you to take the next step.

Shall I edit my manuscript as I write or wait until after it is finished?

To each their own. Some writers wait until they complete their manuscript before beginning the editing process. My style, however, is to edit after writing each section.

As you read in the section "From First Draft to Final Manuscript," after writing each section, I set it aside for twenty-four hours before rereading it. I then send it to my sounding board advisors who share their feedback within seventy-two hours.

After integrating some if not all of their recommendations, I put that section to bed. Once the entire manuscript is finished, I reread the sections in the order that they have been laid out. This is when I make minor modifications, switch sections around, etc.

As I am engaging in this process, I continue to ask myself the question, "Will this *information* help my readers?" As you may guess, the specific question that I asked myself for this book was, "Will the information in this section help to bring out the book inside of the person reading it?"

How do you manage the stress of meeting a book deadline?

When writing my first five books, I was not very much fun to be around. I was raising a family and working ninety-hour weeks. I would write after everyone went to bed. Now that my family is grown, it is much easier to find quiet time to write.

During the last week before a book deadline, I frequently check into a hotel and just write. Those hotel award points definitely come in handy. If staying in a hideaway hotel isn't an alternative for you, find a place where you can concentrate without interruption.

What book genres sell better than others?

Thomas Stewart wrote an article about this very topic for *TheRichest.com.* In his January 31, 2014, piece entitled *Which Five Book Genres Make the Most Money,* the best-selling ones were:

1. Romance/erotica
2. Crime/mystery
3. Religious/inspirational
4. Science fiction and fantasy
5. Horror

Not much has changed during the past five years. These genres continue to be the top selling ones. My recommendation for you, however, is to not limit yourself to what sells the best. Instead, write what you know, what you have experienced, and what you are the most passionate about. By doing so, you will produce your best work. Note: In Spring 2020, I will show you how to make *your* book a top selling one in your genre in my eleventh book, *How to Get Your Book Published and Sell It As Though Your Life Depends On It.* The content of this book will have more value to you only if you already have a book written, so get going.

What are the guidelines for getting permission to quote people in a book?

As a general rule, it is best to obtain permission if you quote 250 words or more in total from one book, or 50 words or more from one magazine, newspaper, journal, or web article.

What is a suggested book length?

It depends on the type of book you are writing. Rather than talking about the length of a book, let's talk about word count.

In the *Writer's Digest* article "Word Count for Novels and Children's Books: The Definitive Post,"[1] Chuck Sambuchino makes the following recommendations:

Sci-fi and fantasy novels: 110,000–115,000 words

Middle-grade fiction: 20,000–55,000 words

Simpler middle-grade idea: 20,000–35,000 words

Young adult fiction: 55,000–79,000 words

Picture books: 500–600 words for a standard thirty-two-page book

Western: 50,000–80,000 words

Memoir: 80,000–89,000 words

Shall I write with the intention of my book being published?

That is your choice. I personally like to write with the goal of writing a book to be published.

Rather than writing with a book as the end result, some writers prefer wading in the writing water before taking the plunge. Some document their thoughts as a form of therapy, and others write for the mere sake of it.

As you read in the section "From Writer to Author: The Steps for Getting There," authors have been known to convert their writing from years past into a book.

Whatever your reason, write. By doing so, you will be acquiring the habit so that when you are ready to bring out the book in you, the writing process will be second nature.

Reflection: Which answer in the above FAQs was of most value to you?

In Retrospect . . .

What Seasoned Authors Would Tell Their Younger Writing Selves

We wrote to taste life twice, in the moment and in retrospect.

—Anaïs Nin

Years ago, I read a line that has stuck with me. It was, "If you were nintey-two, what would you wish you would have done?"

While none of the none authors quoted in this book are ninety-two years young, they sure are sage. You will see what I mean when you read their responses to my question: If they could tell their younger writing selves anything, what would it be?

I hope one or more of their comments will give you a push to bring out that book in you.

If you write about something you know or are passionate about, then you are more than halfway done. Don't be afraid to have your own voice. Stay in the moment and be aware that songs you hear, conversations you have, even your writing environment, all spike your inspiration for writing.
—LISA BARRETTA, AUTHOR,
CONSCIOUS INK: THE HIDDEN MEANING OF TATTOOS

Don't push yourself beyond your limits. The stress of writing is hard enough!

—Dr. Susan A. Berger, author,
The Five Ways We Grieve

When people ask me for advice about writing a first book, I tell them about what I call the three Ps:

Passion: you have an intense interest in the subject matter.

People: there is a big audience to purchase your book.

Persistence: you must keep going forward even if there are setbacks.

—Jan Cullinane, coauthor,
The Single Woman's Guide to Retirement

Stop sitting on those journals. You are sitting on a gold mine.

—Dr. Allana Da Graca, author
Tomorrow Can't Wait: An Inspirational Book Offering Persistence for a Lifetime

If you want to write, write. Read. Write some more. Never be so arrogant as to think you are the greatest writer there ever was. You aren't. Never be so meek to think you are the worst writer, either. You aren't.

—Marie D. Jones, author,
The Disaster Survival Guide: How to Prepare for and Survive Floods, Fires, Earthquakes, and More

Stay curious.

—Maryann Karinch, author,
Telemedicine: What the Future Holds When You're Ill

Write fearlessly. Let it all out.

—Lydia Lambert, author,
Kissing Frogs: The Path to a Prince

Hang in there. It really does happen.
—GAIL Z. MARTIN, AUTHOR,
THE ESSENTIAL SOCIAL MEDIA MARKETING HANDBOOK AND
30 DAYS TO SOCIAL MEDIA SUCCESS

There will be times when you wonder if it is all worth it. I would suggest staying committed. If writing a book were easy, then everybody would be doing it. You've got to forge ahead. I literally wore out a Dell keyboard toward the end of writing my first book.
—KEN MURRAY, AUTHOR, *ON PARR*

Take a chance and start writing. You never know where it will lead you.
—JOHN PIERCE, AUTHOR,
SELL MORE AND SLEEP AT NIGHT: RELATIONSHIPS WITH EMOTIONAL INTELLIGENCE TO INCREASE SALES

You don't win at writing if you have a big book deal at twenty-five. You win at writing by finishing a project well—by taking the time to dive deep into the editing weeds to make every single page, paragraph, and sentence everything it can be. Putting in that work makes you a better writer, so don't for a second feel like you're behind schedule. If you're pushing forward, writing, wordsmithing, reading voraciously, learning about the industry, and befriending others in the writing community, that's winning.
—KRIS SPISAK, AUTHOR, *GET A GRIP ON YOUR GRAMMAR*

Reflection: If you were ninety-two years old and looking back at yourself at this very moment, what would you be telling yourself?

Final Advice to Budding Authors from Those Who Have Written Between One and Seventy-Six Books!

Wise men don't need advice. Fools won't take it.

—Benjamin Franklin

Don't give up! I had many necessary interruptions due to having to work. But I believed in my book and my ability to complete it.

Find the right people to support you, edit, and guide you through the process.

You can't write well if you are not emotionally, mentally, and physically in good shape!

—SUSAN BERGER, AUTHOR, *THE FIVE WAYS WE GRIEVE*

I have found that the areas that become our greatest teachers in life can be found in our deep valleys of pain. Dig deep into your story, and let others know what skills and insights they can learn from what you have to share. Don't let those tears go to waste.

—ALLANA DA GRACA, AUTHOR,
TOMORROW CAN'T WAIT: AN INSPIRATIONAL BOOK OFFERING PERSISTENCE FOR A LIFETIME

Treat your writing like a business. Don't rush; make it your best work. At the same time, know when to let go. At some point, you have to put your "baby" out into the world!

—GAIL Z. MARTIN, AUTHOR,
THE ESSENTIAL SOCIAL MEDIA MARKETING HANDBOOK AND *30 DAYS TO SOCIAL MEDIA SUCCESS*

Make it interesting from the first page.

—HERB REISENFELD, AUTHOR, *CHECKING INN*

Reflection: Which advice will you put into practice?

Epilogue

As I write the last lines of this book, a feeling of sadness sweeps over me. I realize that I will miss hearing and responding to my inner writing voice on a daily basis.

We traveled so many places together to get to this point—the kitchen and dining room tables, hotel desks and lobbies, the "attic" on the 58th floor.

Rather than prolonging this bittersweet moment, my writing voice and I have planned our next journey together: to write *How To Get Your Book Published and Sell It As Though Your Life Depends On It* (release date Spring 2020).

I promised you that I would—and just as I trust you will keep your word with your inner writing voice, I vow to tell you how to take your book to market and make it a winner!

Until then, get ready and get set to begin your writing journey. You too have a built-in travel companion.

Have a Question?

Do you have questions about bringing out the book in you? Remember, the only foolish question is the one you don't ask.

Email: *annmarie@bringoutyourbook.com*

annmarie@annmariesabath.com

Website: *www.bringoutyourbook.com*

www.bringoutyourbook.com/freeresources

www.annmariesabath.com

Text: (513) 200-0449

Twitter: @bringoutyourbo1

https://twitter.com/bringoutyourbo1

@AnnMarieSabath

https://twitter.com/AnnMarieSabath

LinkedIn: *www.linkedin.com/in/everybody-has-a-book-in-side-of-them-2abb37183/*

www.linkedin.com/in/ann-marie-sabath-0262a9/

Facebook: Bring Out Your Book

fb.me/BringOutYourBook

www.facebook.com/AnnMarieSabath/

Instagram: bring_out_your_book

www.instagram.com/bring_out_your_book/

www.instagram.com/ann_marie_sabath/

List of Contributors

Lisa Barretta

Lisa Barretta is a practicing astrologer and a member of the National Council for Geocosmic Research, American Federation of Astrologers, and International Society for Astrological Research. She practices as an intuitive counselor, certified Reiki practitioner, and researcher in the fields of consciousness and psychic sensing.

Lisa is the author of *Conscious Ink: The Hidden Meaning of Tattoos, The Book of Transformation,* and *The Street Smart Psychic's Guide to Getting a Good Reading.* She writes in different genres that include arts and photography; religion and spirituality; health, fitness, and dieting; and self-help.

In addition to being an author, Lisa is also the executive producer for the PBS documentary *Surviving Death: A Paranormal Debate,* featured at the Philip K. Dick Film Festival held in the Williamsburg section of Brooklyn, New York. For more information, visit her website at *www.LisaBarretta.com.*

Susan A. Berger

Susan A. Berger, EdD, LICSW, counsels people who are confronting significant loss and other life changes. She also trains professionals in using her unique approach to helping the bereaved. She has twenty-five years of experience in the health and mental health fields as a researcher, practitioner, administrator, and consultant in both Massachusetts and Washington, DC.

Dr. Berger is the author of *The Five Ways We Grieve: Finding Your Personal Path to Healing After the Loss of a Loved One*. She writes in the health, fitness, and dieting and self-help genres.

Dr. Berger lectures widely in professional healthcare, business, government, and university settings. She has held faculty appointments at three colleges, teaching courses in human behavior and psychology. She has also served as a hospice volunteer. Dr. Berger is herself a survivor of early parental loss. Additional information on Dr. Berger can be found on LinkedIn.

Jan Cullinane

Jan Cullinane is a bestselling and award-winning author, speaker, and consultant. She is featured on TV, radio, and in many newspapers and magazines.

Jan is the author of *The Single Woman's Guide to Retirement, The New Retirement: The Ultimate Guide to the Rest of Your Life,* and *Retire Happy: An Inspiring Guide to the Rest of Your Life. The Single Woman's Guide to Retirement* received a Living Now Book Award, an Apex Award for Publishing Excellence in the books and ebooks category, and a Mature Media Award. She writes in different genres that include travel; business and money; health, fitness, and aging; parenting; and relationships.

Cullinane has a bachelor's and master's degree from the University of Maryland, and is ABD from Rutgers, the State University of New Jersey. She can also speak backward fluently! Visit Jan *at www.JanCullinane.com,* and follow her on Twitter @jancullinane.

Allana Da Graca

Allana Da Graca is the president of Turning On the Lights Global Institute in Boston. She designs personal and professional development products to help individuals win in life. Her seminars include Women Build Confidence, Business Communication Practice and Entrepreneurship, and Social Media Content Design. Allana began writing in 1999 as a student journalist with the UMass Daily Collegian. In 2006, she published her first booklet, *Temple: Self-Discovery Through Truth.*

Allana is the author of *Chronicles of a Poet, Tomorrow Can't Wait: Offering Persistence of a Lifetime,* and the Women Build Confidence Coaching Series. Allana shared that the inspiration for both the confidence-building series and *Chronicles of A Poet* came from the *Green Book.*

She writes in different genres that include literature and fiction, religion and spirituality, and self-help. To learn more about Allana Da Graca, please visit her website at *www.DrAllanaDaGraca.com.*

Cornelia Gamlem

Cornelia Gamlem is an author, consultant, and speaker. She is founder and president of the Gems Group, a management consulting firm that offers human resources and business solutions.

Cornelia is the coauthor of *The Manager's Answer Book, The Big Book of HR, The Conflict Resolution Phrase Book,* and *The Roadmap to Success.* She writes in two different genres that include business, and money and reference.

Cornelia has been quoted in major publications including the *Wall Street Journal, Fortune, the New York Times, Forbes, CEO Magazine, Fast Company,* the *Chicago Tribune,* and *Newsday.* She's been interviewed in major markets around the country and contributed articles to numerous blogs and websites, including *www.FastCompany.com,*

She has also served as a technical editor for McGraw Hill Education and is a member of SouthWest Writers in Albuquerque, New Mexico.

Marie D. Jones

Marie D. Jones is the bestselling author of the EKHO: Evil Kid Hunting Organization middle-grade fiction series, which she wrote with her son, Max Jones, based on his spy group, EKHO, in grade school. She is also the author of the novel *Black Wolf, White Swan.*

Her nonfiction books include *Destiny vs. Choice: The Scientific and Spiritual Evidence Behind Fate and Free Will; PSIence: How New Discoveries in Quantum Physics and New Science May Explain the Existence of Paranormal Phenomena;* and *Supervolcano: The Catastrophic Event that Changed the Course of Human History.* She writes in different genres that include science fiction and fantasy; religion and spirituality; politics and social sciences; science and math; self-help; health, fitness, and dieting; and literature and fiction.

Marie has an extensive background in journalism, metaphysics, and the paranormal, and worked as a field investigator for MUFON (Mutual UFO Network) in the 1980s and 1990s. For more information, her website is *www.MarieDJones.com.*

Maryann Karinch

Maryann Karinch is the author of thirty books, most of which focus on human behavior. In recognition of her work as a dedicated explorer of the psyche, The Explorers Club elected her to membership in March 2010. Maryann frequently shares her expertise in interpersonal management skills with audiences in need of specialized training in those areas.

In 2004, Maryann founded The Rudy Agency, a literary agency specializing in nonfiction. Earlier in her career, she served as PR manager for the Federal Systems Group of Apple Computer and director of communications for a prominent lobbying organization in Washington, DC. She also managed a professional theater in the Nation's Capital. Maryann holds bachelor's and master's degrees in speech and drama from the Catholic University of America in Washington, DC. She is also an American Council on Exercise certified personal trainer and former competitive athlete in gymnastics, endurance racing, and bodybuilding. For more information, visit *www.karinch.com* and *www.RudyAgency.com*.

Lydia Lambert

Lydia Lambert is a retired public school principal and high school English teacher who continues to look for Mr. Right when she isn't traveling the world, playing the piano and golf, and helping others with writing challenges. Lydia resides in Cincinnati, Ohio. As of this printing, Lydia has completed her PhD and is content with her single status.

Gail Z. Martin

Gail Z. Martin is a Penn State MBA in marketing/computer systems who worked for seventeen years as a VP of corporate communications and in other marketing roles before founding DreamSpinner Communications in 2003. She is the author of eight nonfiction books, including *The Essential Social Media Marketing Handbook* and *30 Days to Social Media Success*. *LifeHack* named *30 Days to Social Media Success* as one of the Top 20 Business Books to read in 2016.

Writing as Morgan Brice, Gail is also the bestselling, award-winning author of more than twenty-five fiction novels in epic fantasy, urban fantasy, steampunk, comedic horror, and paranormal romance. She is also an invited contributor to more than forty US/UK anthologies. Follow her fiction at @GailZMartin or @MorganBriceBook and her nonfiction at @GailMartinPR. Find her online for fiction at *www.GailZMartin.com* and *www.MorganBrice.com,* and for nonfiction at *www.DreamSpinnerCommunications.com.*

Barbara Mitchell

Barbara Mitchell is an author, speaker, and the managing partner of The Mitchell Group, a human resources and organizational development consulting practice. Prior to starting her own business, she was in senior leadership positions with Marriott International.

Barbara is the coauthor of *The Big Book of HR, The Essential HR Handbook, The Essential Workplace Conflict Handbook, The Manager's Answer Book,* and *The Conflict Resolution Phrase Book.* She writes in two different genres that include business and money, and reference.

Barbara is a frequent speaker to business groups and has been quoted in the *Wall Street Journal,* the *Financial Times, Forbes,* the *New York Times, Fast Company,* the *Chicago Tribune,* and *Newsday.* She's been interviewed on radio around the United States and contributed to numerous blogs and websites, including *www.Forbes.com, www.inc.com,* and *www.Entrepreneur.com.*

Barbara is an active volunteer who has served on numerous national and local boards and is a video docent at the Smithsonian American Art Museum.

Ken Murray

Ken Murray's first book, *On Parr,* was published in February 2018 following his twenty-five-year career in the United

States Air Force from which he retired as a lieutenant colonel.

Ken graduated with a bachelor's degree in public relations with a journalism minor from the University of Northern Iowa in 1985 followed by joining the Air Force in 1986, where he earned his MBA in 1990 from the University of South Dakota.

Besides spending many years as an instructor navigator at the Nav School at Randolph Air Force Base in Texas, Ken was a combat veteran who flew missions in support of Operations Just Cause, Desert Storm, and Allied Force, and was chief of combat operations at the Combined Air Operations Center at Al Udeid AB, Qatar, supporting Iraqi Freedom and Enduring Freedom.

Ken had publishing in his bloodline. He was an understudy at Hudson Printing Company in Hudson, Iowa, owned and operated by his parents for more than forty-nine years.

Erica Orloff

Erica Orloff is the author of over twenty novels for adults and young adults, and as Erica Kirov, middle-grade readers. She is a native New Yorker but currently resides in Virginia with her family and menagerie of pets. Despite venturing south, she still roots for the Yankees. In her nonexistent free time, she enjoys knitting, gardening, and hunting for Buddha statues for her collection.

Follow Erica on Twitter @ericaorloff.

John Pierce

John Pierce is head of recruiting for Stifel, a 128-year old wealth management firm. He has an extensive track record of superior results across multidiscipline wealth management divisions of employee and independent firms in the services industry. He consistently demonstrates the ability to produce results in cross-business partnerships. John has superior communication, interpersonal, and communication skills, and the ability to form strong, lasting relationships with clients and coworkers.

John resides in Philadelphia and has competed eleven full-distance Ironman races. Additional information on John can be found on LinkedIn, Facebook, or Twitter.

Herb Reisenfeld

For over forty-three years, Herb Reisenfeld has traveled with thousands of guests all over the United States and many parts of the world. He gets a tremendous thrill sharing his experiences by visiting various destinations that he has been blessed to enjoy many times.

A professional travel agent is experienced to not only provide the service of booking air, hotels, cruises, resorts, etc., but also offer suggestions for special restaurants, guides, excursions, and other unique opportunities beyond just being an order taker.

Herb always ends his trips by asking, "What was your favorite thing about this trip? Was it the hotel, the sights, the food, the other traveling companions?" The correct answer is all the above wrapped up in just one word: "Memories." These last forever! Many of those memories are shared in his book, *Checking Inn*.

Kris Spisak

Kris Spisak wrote her first book, *Get a Grip on Your Grammar: 250 Writing and Editing Reminders for the Curious or Confused* (Career Press, 2017), with the goal to help writers of all kinds sharpen their craft and empower their communications.

Her *Words You Should Know* podcast and Grammartopia events follow the same mission. A former college writing instructor, having taught at institutions including the University of Richmond and Virginia Commonwealth University,

Kris now works as a ghostwriter and freelance editor. She is on the board of directors of James River Writers, is the cofounder/director of creative strategy of Midlothian Web Solutions, and is looking forward to sharing details of her next books (fiction and nonfiction) soon.

To learn more about Kris, visit *www.Kris-Spisak.com.*

Recommended Reading

Aaron, Rachel. *2,000 to 10,000: How to Write Faster, Write Better, and Write More of What You Love*. Aaron/Bach, 2012.

Hanika, Tanja. *Writer's Workbook: A Personal Planner with Tips, Checklists and Guidelines*. CreateSpace Independent Publishing, 2017.

Kelly, Erika. *Build-a-Book: A Prewriting Process*. EK Publishing LLC, 2018.

King, Stephen. *On Writing: A Memoir of the Craft*. Scribner, 2010.

MacDonald, Morgan Gist. *Start Writing Your Book Today: A Step-By-Step Plan to Write Your Nonfiction Book, from First Draft to Finished Manuscript*. Paper Raven Books, 2015.

Nelson, Stacy. *Writing the Damn Book: How To Start, Write and Publish a Non-Fiction Book for Creative People Who Have a Hard Time Finishing Things*. BadAss Publishing Co., 2016.

Serravallo, Jennifer. *The Writing Strategies Book: Your Everything Guide to Developing Skilled Writers*. Heinemann, 2017.

Tracy, Brian. *20-Step Author Quick Start Guide*. Brian Tracy International, 2018.

Zinsser, William. *On Writing Well: The Classic Guide to Writing Nonfiction*. Harper Perennial, 2016.

Recommended Resources

If you have not figured it out throughout this book, my goal is to give you the confidence to bring out that book inside of you. No matter what genre you choose, below are some terrific resources for keeping you motivated on your book-writing journey.

20-Step Author Quick Start Guide

www.briantracy.com/success/how-to-write-a-book/
If you love Brian Tracy's other books, you will love this quick-start guide. Besides getting pumped up to bring out that book in you, you will read several quotes about people who made it happen.

WRITING PODCASTS

Dead Robots' Society

www.deadrobotssociety.com
A great site for aspiring writers. Besides podcasts, aspiring writers will find author interviews, writing tips, book reviews, guest blogs, and more.

Grammar Girl Quick and Dirty Tips for Better Writing

www.quickanddirtytips.com

Mignon Fogarty is the founder of this podcast network that has been named one of *Writer's Digest's* best websites for writers multiple times. You will love this site!

Helping Writers Become Authors

www.helpingwritersbecomeauthors.com/podcasts
K. M. Weiland created this podcast to assist writers in writing their best books. If you are interested in writing a novel, Weiland's site offers tips on how to write it, the way to structure your story, how to write character arcs, and structure scenes. It even shares common writing mistakes. See you there!

I Should Be Writing

www.podtail.com/podcast/i-should-be-writing/
This is a terrific podcast for wannabe fiction writers. New authors will learn how to rev up their writing careers. Episodes typically feature an interview with an author who has a new book.

WRITING WORKSHOPS

The Write Workshops

www.thewriteworkshops.com
If you live in the NYC area and are looking for an in-person workshop where you will be coached as you write, this is a great choice. The classes are limited to six fiction and/or nonfiction writers who receive critiques from publishing professionals and fellow participants. Located in Manhattan, East 35th Street.

WRITING WEBSITES

National Novel Writing Month

www.nanowrimo.org
If you are willing to commit to writing 50,000 words in the thirty days of November, this is the site for you! When you sign on, you will receive the NaNoWriMo Survival Guide presented by BookBaby.

Productive Writer

www.authorguides.com
A terrific online resource by Tim Grahl and Jeff Goins. The course has been designed to help budding authors create the right mindset to write, and then find the time to write.

www.goinswriter.com
Jeff Goins is a master at getting writers psyched. He is the author of five books, including *The Art of Work* and *Real Artists Don't Starve*. In addition, Jeff has many resources to share with budding writers. I especially love his bonus item, "The Writer's Manifesto."

The Creative Penn

www.thecreativepenn.com
From how to create an author mindset to how to write a novel or nonfiction, and even making a living from writing, you will love Joanna Penn's advice.

The Write Life

www.thewritelife.com
You will absolutely love this website. It is filled with writing retreats and conferences, gifts for writers, writing residencies, writing contests, and much more. It is so addictive

that you may have to limit the amount of time you spend on it, or you will not be writing that book inside of you!

WRITERS' GROUPS/CONFERENCES

James River Writers

www.jamesriverwriters.org
The mission of James River Writers is to build a community by connecting and inspiring writers and all those in central Virginia with a love for the written word.

Writer's Digest

www.writersdigest.com
This is the number-one resource for writers. It celebrates the writing life and what it means to be a writer in today's publishing environment.

List of Conferences and Workshops in North America

www.tckpublishing.com/list-of-writers-conferences

https://thejohnfox.com/2016/07/writing-conferences-conventions-workshops/

Notes

Are You Ever Too Young or Too Old to Write a Book?

1. "Writers and Authors: Diversity," *https://datausa.io/profile/soc/273043/#demographics*

2. "8-Year-Old Anaya Lee Willabus Is the Youngest Published Female Author of a Chapter Book in the U.S." June 30, 2015. *https://guyanesegirlsrock.com/8-year-old-anaya-lee-willabus-youngest-published-female-author-chapter-book-u-s/*

3. Guinness World Records. "Oldest Author to Have First Book Published." *www.guinnessworldrecords.com/world-records/oldest-author-to-have-first-book-published*

From Writer to Author: The Steps for Getting There

1. According to Wikipedia, *Green Book* was originated and published by New York City mailman Victor Hugo Green from 1936 to 1966, during the era of Jim Crow laws, when open and often legally prescribed discrimination against nonwhites was widespread. Wikipedia, "Victor Hugo Green," *https://en.wikipedia.org/wiki/Victor_Hugo_Green*

What Is Your Excuse?

1. Top Results Academy. "Brian Tracy Biography." *https://topresultsacademy.com/authors/brian-tracy/biography/*

How to Identify the Book Inside of You

1. Justine Tal Goldberg. *200 Million Americans Want to Publish Books, But Can They?* Publishing Perspectives. May 26, 2011. *https://publishingperspectives. com/2011/05/200-million-americans-want-to-publish-books/*

Are You a Pantser or a Plotter?

1. Cindi Myers. "Plotter or Pantser: The Best of Both Worlds." *AutoCrit*, October 23, 2012. *www.autocrit. com/editing/library/plotter-or-pantser-the-best-of-both-worlds/*

2. Myers, "Plotter or Pantser."

3. David Fernandez. *Becoming a Storyteller: Plotter vs. Pantser, or, Did Stephen King Really Just Call Me a Dullard?* March 2, 2013. *https://bydlfernandez. com/2013/03/02/becoming-a-storyteller-plotter-vs-pantser-or-did-stephen-king-really-just-call-me-a-dullard/*

4. Dorothy Wickenden. "David Remnick Interviews Lee Child, the Creator of Jack Reacher." *The New Yorker, Politics and More Podcast.* August 13, 2018. *www. newyorker.com/podcast/political-scene/david-remnick-interviews-lee-child-the-creator-of-jack-reacher*

Two Ways to Stay Motivated to Write

1. The carrot-and-stick approach is a motivational theory by Jeremy Bentham. This English philosopher, whose ideas were developed around 1800, considered that all people are self-interested and are motivated by the desire to avoid pain and find pleasure. August 15, 2013. *www.indiagk.net/2013/08/carrot-and-stick-theory-by-jeremy.html*

2. The KITA acronym was created by Frederick Herzberg in 1959. The American psychologist became one of the most influential names in business management. As cited by NetMBA Business Knowledge Center, *www.netmba.com/mgmt/ob/motivation/herzberg*

Writing Fitness: How to Stir Up Your Imagination

1. Zoe Henry. "6 Companies (Including Uber) Where It's OK to Nap." *Inc. www.inc.com/zoe-henry/google-uber-and-other-companies-where-you-can-nap-at-the-office.html*

Six Things NOT to Do with Your Manuscript

1. Yohana Desta. "10 Famous Writers Who Don't Use Modern Tech to Create." *Mashable,* February 15, 2014. *https://mashable.com/2014/02/15/modern-writers-technology/#mqyd9KMqzuqF*

2. Frank McNally. "Of Mice and Derrymen: John Steinbeck's Irish Heritage." *Irish Times,* December 19, 2018. *www.irishtimes.com/opinion/of-mice-and-derrymen-john-steinbeck-s-irish-heritage-1.3737290*

3. John Ezard. "The Story of Dr. Jekyll, Mr. Hyde and Fanny, the Angry Wife Who Burned the First Draft." *The Guardian,* October 24, 2000. *www.theguardian.com/uk/2000/oct/25/books.booksnews*

4. Simon Griffin. "10 Books That Have Been Lost to History." *Listverse,* October 8, 2017. *http://listverse.com/2017/10/08/10-books-that-have-been-lost-to-history/*

5. Emily Burnham. "Stephen King 'Horrified' by Loss of His Manuscripts in Bookstore Flooding." *Bangor Daily News*, January 17, 2018. *https://bangordailynews.com/2018/01/17/arts-culture/stephen-king-horrified-by-loss-of-his-manuscripts-in-bookstore-flooding/*

6. John Mullan. "Top 10 Trivia: Lost Manuscripts." *The Guardian,* January 23, 2009. *www.theguardian.com/books/2009/jan/23/1000-novels-lost-manuscripts*

7. Carolyn See. Book review: "The Michener Book That Almost Wasn't: *My Lost Mexico: The Making of a Novel,* by James A. Michener." January 25, 1993. *www.articleslatimes.com http://articles.latimes.com/1993-01-25/news/vw-1613_1_james-michener*

Your Name or a Pen Name?

1. "Pen Names II." *Writer's Relief.* February 13, 2009. *http://writersrelief.com/2009/02/13/pen-names-ii/*

What Makes Authors Write in More Than One Genre?

1. Sadie Trombetta. "13 Bestselling Authors Who Write In More Than One Genre, Including J.K. Rowling, Stephen King, And Neil Gaiman." *Bustle, www.bustle.com/p/13-bestselling-authors-who-write-in-more-than-one-genre-including-jk-rowling-stephen-king-neil-gaiman-2969009*

Fourteen Budding Author FAQ's

1. Chuck Sambuchino. "Word Count for Novels and Children's Books: The Definitive Post." *Writer's Digest,* October 24, 2016. *www.writersdigest.com/editor-blogs/guide-to-literary-agents/word-count-for-novels-and-childrens-books-the-definitive-post*

Other Books by
Ann Marie Sabath

Business Etiquette In Brief

Beyond Business Casual: What to Wear to Work If You Want to Get Ahead

Business Etiquette: 101 Ways to Conduct Business with Charm and Savvy

International Business Etiquette—Asia and the Pacific Rim

International Business Etiquette—Europe

International Business Etiquette—Latin America

Courting Business: 101 Ways for Accelerating Business Relationships

One Minute Manners: Quick Solutions to the Most Awkward Situations You'll Ever Face at Work

What Self-Made Millionaires Do That Most People Don't: 52 Ways to Create Your Own Success